CONT

A YEAR IN THE TRAP GROUNDS

Sketch map of the Trap Grounds

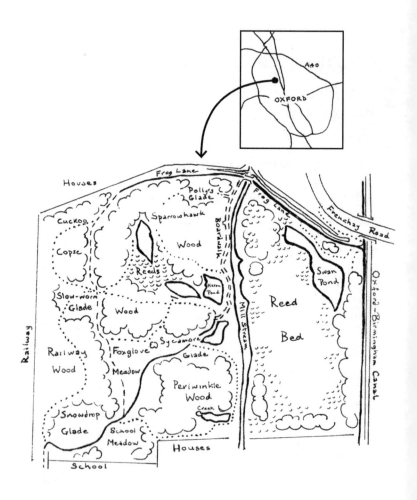

THE TRAP GROUNDS NATURE RESERVE

*Making space for nature
in north Oxford*

ALAN ALLPORT

Published by Alan Allport Publications
24 Merrivale Square, Oxford, OX2 6QX

© Alan Allport 2022

ISBN 978-1-3999-1747-6

Designed and typeset by Steve Mead Graphic Design, Oxford
Cover photograph of a Reed Warbler by Nicola Devine

FOREWORD

It's an early spring morning. I am walking along the canal towpath; birds chirrup; the sky is blue. Across the Oxford Canal, the willows in the back gardens cascade with fresh translucent green. On my left, through a tangle of willows I catch glimpses of a reedbed. Above my head a cock chaffinch shouts his cheerful greeting to the world.

I swing left into Frog Lane - the aptly named entrance to the **Trap Grounds Nature Reserve**. Here, in the watery ditch that runs beside the lane, the frogs have their annual mating frenzy. Pollarded willows lean across it, mirrored in the still water.

Not far off I hear a robin's sweet song, a great tit chanting "teacher, teacher", a wren's even louder trill, their songs reaching me from the willow-carr on my left, where the winter floods still lie. I turn left along a boardwalk that winds its way beside a slow-moving stream, bordered on the far side by a reedbed. A mother duck gently chivvies her ducklings together, lest they stray too far.

I come to a pond on my right, surrounded by leaning willows. A curving wattle fence keeps toddlers from tumbling over the steep bank into the pond. Fifty yards on, the boardwalk curves away from the stream, and we have reached another small pond. The shiny yellow flowers of Marsh Marigold crowd the water's edge. The slope beyond is starry with primroses.

Walking on, I follow a winding path through a succession of three small wildflower meadows, each one bordered with woodland, each with a different flora soon to appear. At this early season it's the modest primroses and celandines, a flush of cowslips and a patch of white violets. Here and there Wild Cherry trees scatter their blossom on the grass.

Everywhere, there is new life.

❋ ❋ ❋

Why does this place enfold me in such enchantment? When I stop for a while to listen to the birds' delightful chatter, to observe the wildflowers, the ever-changing reflections on the water… my mood lightens. I feel a lifting of the heart. Sometimes it is a much stronger feeling. My small self dissolves into a wider being. I *am* the meadow, the stream, the reedbed, and all their myriad inhabitants; there is no longer a boundary between them and me. I am a part of them, and they are a part of me.

How can I share this exhilarating and liberating experience? This little book is my attempt to do so.

A BRIEF HISTORY

Catherine Robinson writes: The Trap Grounds were acquired by St John's College, presumably as a speculative venture, at some point after the completion of the Oxford Canal in 1790. However, the site was never developed for industrial or residential purposes, perhaps because of its tendency to flood. Instead it was used by the college as a rubbish dump until it was sold to Oxford City Council in 1965. For the next 30 years it remained as waste ground and – despite its on-going use as an unofficial fly-tipping site – it gradually evolved into a haven for wildlife: glow worms, lizards, orchids, and much more.

In 1996 I began mobilising local volunteers to clear paths and glades in the woodland and eradicate invasive willows from the reed bed. When the site was earmarked for development in the draft Local Plan for Oxford (2001–2016), we argued that it should be exempted on account of its value for wildlife and community recreation. When this objection was rejected, we launched a campaign to claim the site as a Town Green.

After a public inquiry held in Oxford in 2002, the Inspector, Vivian Chapman QC, accepted our evidence that the western half of the site (the scrubland and woodland) had been used by the local community for lawful pastimes such as dog-walking and birdwatching *as of right* for at least 20 years, and that, in accordance with the Commons Registration Act 1965, it should therefore be registered as a Town Green.

That was not the end of the matter. The case was referred to the High Court in London, where Mr Justice Lightman ruled in our favour. But then the Court of Appeal found against us on a technicality which would have made it virtually impossible for any piece of land anywhere in the country to be registered as a town or village green in future. So we appealed to the House of Lords in 2006 – and won. The law relating to town and village greens was clarified and strengthened by this historic verdict — for six years, at least. Crucial changes were introduced by the Tory government in 2013, when the Growth and Infrastructure Act made it impossible to register land as a town or village green if the land has been earmarked (however tentatively) for planning and development. But the western half of the Trap Grounds is safe from development in perpetuity.

Although we represented ourselves in the early stages of the town green campaign and hired a young barrister for a fixed fee at the later stages, the entire campaign cost us £50,000, which was made possible by the generosity of local supporters, and the proceeds of concerts in church halls and street stalls selling second-hand books. The texts of the verdicts can be read on our website (www.trap-grounds.org. uk).

After the western section of the Trap Grounds was registered as a Town Green in 2007, the eastern section was classified by the County Council as a Local Wildlife Site in 2010. This designation was extended to the western half in 2015. The whole site remains in the ownership of the City

Council and is now officially managed by the Friends in partnership with the Council.

RE-WILDING AN
OXFORD FLY-TIP

Past and Present

When I first discovered the Trap Grounds, in the early 1980s, it was a startlingly different place, into which few cared to venture. Much of it was an impenetrable jungle of brambles higher than my head, frequented by occasional rough sleepers and drug users. It had become a casual rubbish dump. Fly-tipping continued until at least 1996, when local volunteers – inspired by Catherine Robinson - began to reclaim it as a wildlife site.

The legacy of those earlier years was the discarded rubbish of an industrialised world: hundreds of worn-out car tyres, steel reinforcing rods bent into surreal entanglements, galvanised iron cisterns, heaps of shattered glass and pottery, and countless piles of broken bricks. Frog Lane was blocked by an abandoned caravan minus its wheels. You stumbled over unravelling coils of barbed wire, a whole truck chassis, and cartloads upon cartloads of smashed bottles.

The three-acre reedbed was there, with the swampy willow-carr adjoining it, and a barely discernible, silted-up stream. Scores of young willows had invaded the reedbed, which was on the way to drying out and turning into another bit of scrub woodland. Elsewhere there were thickets of hawthorn, and densely shaded stands of sycamores. Little else looked anything like it does today. There were no ponds, no paths (besides the half-blocked Frog Lane), no boardwalk. What are now flowering meadows were thorny scrub and a maze of fallen trees.

❋ ❋ ❋

Catherine Robinson has described, above, how she rescued this site from the developers, in a heroic legal campaign lasting five long years, all the way to the House of Lords. The existence of this green oasis on the edge of North Oxford is owed entirely to her tireless persistence and resolve. We owe her an immense debt of gratitude, both for the legal campaign, *and* for her invaluable work as Secretary of the Friends of the Trap Grounds.

Thank you, Catherine!

TRANSFORMATION
Part of my own enjoyment of the Trap Grounds comes from witnessing – and contributing to – its gradual transformation,

over the past quarter century, from a junk-encumbered waste ground into what it is now: a rich and varied haven for wildlife and – increasingly - a valued resource for local people. Year by year, the junk has been gathered up by dedicated volunteers, and transported – in thousands of wheelbarrow loads - to the canal-side entrance, and from there up the steep ramp to skips beside Frenchay Road. How many skips have we filled over that 25-year period? I have not kept count.

We have felled a few of the tall trees that overshaded the meadows; and we have planted nearly 500 other, mostly smaller trees and flowering shrubs. We have installed the boardwalk, and created a network of footpaths around the site. We have excavated the ponds and dredged the stream, sculpting the banks and planting water's-edge wildflowers and ferns. We have cleared the meadows of fallen trees and scrub, uprooting thousands of brambles, sowing wildflowers in their place.

Today the Trap Grounds includes a wide variety of wildlife habitats within its mere ten acres. We benefit from being close to – indeed part of – the Thames flood plain. In winter, across nearly half the site, you need only dig down a foot or two before you reach the water table. Over the years we have exploited this fact to create our six ponds, each one distinct in character, each, in turn, favoured by a different suite of watery wildlife.

And the furure?

As I write, we are in the second year of a global **Coronavirus pandemic**. Everyone's life has been disrupted, turned upside down. Too many of us have lost friends or family members to the deadly Covid virus. For over a year, with travel and social contact radically restricted, we worked from home, home-educated our kids, becoming dependent on Zoom or other digital media for practically all our human interactions outside our own four walls.

One of the paradoxical side-effects of being 'locked-down' for so long is the powerful need to be *outside*, away from the confines of those four walls; and – whenever possible – immersed in a living green environment. For many people, this has been a novel discovery, or at least a radical *re*-discovery. What an uplift of mood, a renewal of energy can come from being surrounded by nature, from being among trees or by water, hearing birdsong, finding a flowering meadow.

The Trap Grounds nature reserve has witnessed this effect dramatically, with a huge increase in visitor numbers. I frequently meet people who tell me this is their first visit, or that they have only recently heard about the site, or newly discovered it for themselves. And then they come back again. And again. They bring their children, their grandchildren.

That, to me, is the most important development of all. Acquaintance with the living world is urgently needed, for both young and old. In May 2021, we hosted a visit to the Trap Grounds by a group of Oxford University biology students. Catherine Robinson and I took them on a guided tour of the site, telling them about some of its history, its flora and fauna, its conservation management. But I am struck by how little these bright young students are familiar with even our commonest wildlife. I ask them, 'What's that songbird?' (A wren.) They have no idea. That butterfly? A shrug, a wry smile, a shake of the head. Marsh Marigolds, in full flower? Not one of the students can name them. And they don't look about them; they have not yet learned to be alert to their living surroundings. While the group was gathering beside the canal, a magnificent pair of Sparrowhawks circled above our heads for several minutes, calling. Later, I asked whether any of the students had seen or heard them. The answer was: not one.

These intellectually-gifted biology students have learned about DNA and protein structures and genomics – stuff they read about in textbooks; but they are ignorant – and seemingly oblivious – of so much of the living world all around them. How much they miss! And how deep has become their separation from the non-human natural world, cut off from it behind computer and television screens.

In the small Cotswold village where I grew up in the 1940s, my playmates – the children of farm labourers – were familiar with hundreds of plants and animals. That was before the era of television, let alone the era of social media and the internet; before the era in which – without meaning to – humanity launched its all-out onslaught on natural eco-systems and a stable climate.

On the trajectory that humanity is pursuing, those things cannot last. We are on the verge of losing this most bounteous of worlds, this unique miracle in the universe, our earthly paradise. If we are lucky, we have perhaps one more human generation before climate refugees are fleeing in their millions: fleeing from eco-system collapse; from rising seas, from terrible droughts and famine, from wildfires and unbearable heatwaves. Before the resource wars overwhelm us.

The scientists have made all this abundantly clear. Our current economic system, like a cancer, can only keep growing. With just 3% annual growth, our economic footprint – that is, the using-up and destruction of the living world – doubles roughly every 20 years. At that rate, in 100 years from now our destructive footprint would be 32 times greater than it is today; except that, long before then, it will have triggered the collapse of our life-support systems .

How have we allowed this to happen: sleepwalking into climate catastrophe and eco-system collapse? In part, I believe, it is because we have become so cut off from the natural world. To us in our wealthy, urban world, surrounded by technology and concrete, enclosed in cars and aeroplanes, nature has become almost invisible.

That's why I am happy that many more people now choose to visit the Trap Grounds. And to bring their children. Perhaps to re-connect: to sleep-walk no longer.

THIS LITTLE BOOK

What follows is a diary of one year in the Trap Grounds: 2021. It records, month by month, the seasonal changes in the living world; encounters with its wildlife, the plants and animals that live there; and the work done round the year by the **Friends of the Trap Grounds**, and many others, to conserve and enhance it.

I hope it will be of interest to anyone who knows and loves this little oasis, and that it may encourage you to look after it for the future.

*All **line drawings** are by the author. Many of them are based on – and inspired by – photographs by Nicola Devine, with her kind permission.*

A YEAR IN THE TRAP GROUNDS

JANUARY

New Year 2021. Fog rolls across the reedbed. Last year's reeds stand bowed under its weight; every seed-head loaded down with dewdrops. Our three acres of reedbed are flooded above the top of my wellies.

The first few weeks of January are the nadir of the year. Life is at its lowest ebb. On days of dense cloud – that is, most days – twilight begins by 4 pm. They are hungry days and long cold nights for wildlife.

Twice recently I have met a **young Fox** trotting across the meadow in the half-light. The first time, he came within a few yards of me before stopping. He sniffed inquiringly, circled me once right around; then sat down and scratched for a while, still looking at me. I remained still as a bush. After a few minutes he nodded at me and trotted off calmly into the dark woodland. It felt like a kind of greeting, an acceptance. "I'm OK, You're OK."

Throughout last December it rained torrentially. The stream and all our six ponds rose one foot, then another foot, then another, flooding across their banks, extending into all the neighbouring swampy woodlands. The floods remain. Today it looks more like Amazonia than Oxfordshire. After last year's dredging, organised by the Friends of the Trap Grounds, Frog Lane ditch is filled with clear water, in which the aged willow pollards that lean over it are beautifully reflected.

From December's incessant rain, the well-used paths through the Trap Grounds have turned into standing puddles and slippery mud, through which people skid and squelch, puddles beloved by small kids in wellies – less so by their parents.

We order 2.5 tons of limestone gravel. Twelve stalwart volunteers trundle it in groaning wheelbarrow-loads to where it can be spread along the main path. Soon we have used up all the gravel, spreading it to recreate a narrow walkway, firm and dry underfoot. The many other paths, just as squelchy, will have to wait their turn. There is only so much that our volunteer labour-force can undertake in one day.

I make a sad discovery: a full-grown fox, dead, the corpse sprawled beneath low branches, his haunch chewed to the bone. Was he cornered by one or more of the many big dogs allowed by their owners to roam, unleashed, through the Trap Grounds every day, despite notices with a polite request: *"Please keep your dog on a lead"*?

How sad that this can occur within these precious ten acres. It's a *nature reserve*, not a space in which dogs are free to run riot. We are delighted to welcome people **and** their dogs, to visit and enjoy the natural world that we work so hard to protect. But not at the price of harassing to death its wild inhabitants!

WATER, AND WATER VOLES

Since the Mill Stream was dredged for the second time, last October, it has turned into a long narrow lake stretching beside and beyond the boardwalk. The opposite shore is lined with steep banks, where the dredger deposited the dark sludgy spoil from the stream bed. Before the dredger came, we commissioned the ever-resourceful Oxford Conservation Volunteers to build us a wattle fence along the water's edge, to hold back the almost liquid sludge. They hammered six-foot-long stakes deep into the bank, weaving hundreds of slender willow wands between the stakes, to create a kind of sieve through which, later, the black water poured, leaving behind a steep bank that has now firmed up. In due course the willow wands will rot away. Our hope is that one day these waterside banks will become home to families of Water Voles – once those timid creatures have found their way safely there.

A generation or two ago, Water Voles were abundant, to be seen on the banks of every lowland water-course in England. But, within a few decades, their population plummeted. American Mink had escaped from their fur-farm prisons, and spread rapidly; thousands more captive Mink were released by Animal Rights activists. And these alien Mink, invading every waterway, have killed Water Voles in their millions, until, today, a bare 2 or 3 per cent of their former numbers remain.

But there is hope. Since Otter hunting was banned, Otters have returned to many of the streams and rivers of southern England. They are even occasionally sighted along the Oxford canal; and they sometimes leave signs of their presence in the Trap Grounds. And wherever Otters encounter Mink, the Mink are driven away. As rival predators, Mink are not tolerated anywhere within the Otters' territory. Today, the upper Thames catchment is an Otter stronghold; Mink have largely disappeared from the area; and at last Water Vole populations are beginning to recover.

WINTER WEATHER UPS AND DOWNS

Not yet the 10th of January, but already the first snowdrops are pushing up through the rain-softened soil, showing in dense clusters of slender green spires. Any day now, they could be in flower. And as I gently brush aside the carpets of dead leaves, rosettes of primrose leaves are revealed.

In mid-January, we have three days of warm sunlight. I can feel the warmth on my back, on my face. It's a novel sensation, after weeks of cloud, cold, and wet. Like us, the birds respond to the sun's unaccustomed warmth. Thrushes have begun singing from their tree-top vantage points; Robins are active; Wrens are trilling from their ivy-clad tree boles. From time to time I hear the vigorous drumming of a Green Woodpecker, beating out his territory. "Spring is on the way", they are all saying, "Time to get busy, time to mark out my feeding territory, this year's nesting domain." Plants, too. In a few sheltered places Snowdrops have opened in showy clusters, although most are still asleep, eyes tight shut. Occasionally, queen bumble bees can be seen, prospecting for a nest site.

Overhead, after months of grey overcast, the skies are indescribably beautiful. Isolated clouds forever changing, in colours ranging from brilliant white through grey, mauve, purple, and black, drift across a pale blue dome. On the Thames, not far away, two pairs of Goosanders are performing synchronised diving. A swift leap and a plunge, staying underwater for 60 seconds or more, all four reappearing together. After the December rains, the swirling current sweeps them downstream. Underwater they must swim against the flow, to break the surface upstream from where they last disappeared. Both male and female are resplendent in their contrasted plumage: the female redheaded with a splendid backward-pointing crest that she flicks up and down, white throat, blue-grey flanks. The male has a glossy, green-black head, bright white flanks. Male and female both have the distinctive red 'saw-bill' with serrated teeth for grasping fish. There, up comes a goosander with a fish, which he deftly swallows.

❀ ❀ ❀

After three balmy winter days, towards evening a new weather pattern appears: immensely tall clouds, streaked vertically, moving in from the north – a sign of snow. At the same time, in the south-west, a raging sunset of scarlet and gold, lighting the bare willow branches in a smoky orange glow. Overnight a deep frost, and in the morning **snow**, piled on every branch, blankets the ground. Pristine, still untrampled, the snow is utterly beautiful. But no good for planting! We had planned a work party for the coming Sunday afternoon, to plant out 200 spring bulbs in Railway Wood. A dozen eager volunteers had signed up for it. A hasty phone call with Catherine, and we have postponed the work party. I am free to wander among this magical white wilderness. Even among the drifted snow, the snowdrops still raise their delicate heads, defiantly, in compact clumps.

Over the next few days, several stout snowmen appear, standing guard over the meadows. One has a battered saucepan for a hat, a pink scarf around his neck. Families have glorious snowball fights.

In the last week of January, the weather swings again: torrential rain for two days and two nights. The ground, already saturated, can absorb no more. The Thames, the Cherwell, and every other waterway in Oxfordshire has become a churning brown torrent, spreading far beyond their accustomed banks. Port Meadow, the ancient common grazing land for the city, is a shining lake two miles long, all the way to Wolvercote.

In the Trap Grounds, the ponds have overspilled their banks. The path that skirts the Dragonfly Pool has vanished. Even in tall wellies you can scarcely get by. A section of the boardwalk is under water. And once more the footpaths, wherever we have not spread fresh gravel, are slick with treacherous mud.

Creating a newt creek

On the far side of the stream, towards its southern end, is an area of wet woodland. It's a secluded corner, well protected from human incursion, frequented by Moorhens, Herons, occasional Water Voles. Spotted Woodpeckers nest in the big sprawling willows.

On the nearer, west bank, what we call Periwinkle Wood extends along the southern edge of the site, adjoining Navigation Way. For years it was a no-go area, practically impenetrable. Head-high bramble thickets among fallen willows; beneath the brambles, countless piles of rubbish. Self-seeded trees – Sycamore, Ash, Hawthorn, Chestnut – spread their branches high overhead. In places, blue-flowered Periwinkle sprawl among the brambles – hence the name of this secluded corner. This exquisite form of Periwinkle is *Vinca major hirsuta*, a less common variety, presumably a long-ago garden escape, or maybe a relic of the days when St John's College used the area as a dumping ground. Purists may say that we should eradicate all cultivated plants from the Trap Grounds, but it could be argued that they are part of the unique history of the site, and should be allowed to flourish.

Within this jungle, not far from the stream, we uncovered a narrow, winding gully, some twenty yards long, in winter filled with water. Like the rest of Periwinkle Wood, the gully was encumbered by piles of broken bricks, discarded cisterns, tangled iron rods. For some years Catherine and I had dreamed of one day dragging out this junk; then deepening the gully enough to be water-filled all year, creating a little creek. In our dream, the creek would be surrounded by ferns, wild garlic, other waterside plants. We imagined it as – one day – a haven for newts and other minibeasts, free from predation by fish because not connected to the stream.

Starting around 2016, we took the first steps to realise that little dream. We commissioned the Oxford Conservation Volunteers (OCV) to remove the worst of the junk. They dragged out huge iron water-tanks; steel reinforcing-rods thicker than your thumb, twisted into two-metre tangles; a whole truck-chassis. We had no way of transporting these monsters without first chopping them into smaller, more manageable pieces. Enter Phil Hunter of OCV, with his angle grinder. A noisy, ill-tempered beast, the angle grinder; but Phil did a magnificent job with it. Now at last we could load the segmented iron pieces onto wheelbarrows and trundle them laboriously to the canal-side entrance, eventually to pile them into innumerable skips.

In 2017 we received an unexpected offer from Network Rail contractors, working on the nearby line: a day's volunteer work-party – including machinery. At our request they brought in a digger, and part-excavated the gully, while other of their volunteers dug tree planting holes. Useful work! But during a long dry spell that summer the gully almost dried out again. They had not dug deep enough. So Tim Wray, skilled operator of all kinds of diggers, was brought in. Tim has excavated several of our other ponds for us. His big machine dug down, deeper and wider, flinging aside masses of silt and yet more man-made junk. And as he dug, the water poured in.

Now we had the bare outlines of our dreamed-of creek, lined with steep banks, and filled with clear water all year. But the digging had generated another problem, one all-too familiar to us. Beside the winding creek we now had masses of excavated brick rubble, broken bottles, bedsprings, metal drainpipes. Once more our faithful TG volunteers came to the rescue. They gathered up the metal, ceramics, and broken glass, and carried them – in scores of swaying, heavily loaded wheelbarrow trips – to the canal entrance. We ordered yet another skip.

The shattered bricks, tipped everywhere, were a different problem. The creative solution, as in other parts of the site, was to turn them into a feature of the landscape: piled into two long mounds a little way from the creek side, eventually to be covered with several tons of topsoil. Like the gravel, we get the topsoil delivered over the Navigation Way fence, in one-ton bags, right next to where it is needed. Once more we call on the Oxford Conservation Volunteers with their shovels and their muscle power and enthusiasm for hard labour, to gather the brick rubble into two compact mounds and then spread the topsoil generously over them.

At last the creek is taking shape, albeit as yet a bare, mud-covered shape. We begin transplanting ferns – Hart's-tongue and Male ferns – from other parts of the site and replanting them on the topsoil-covered mounds. Generous supporters donate more ferns from their gardens. On the north side of the creek, where much of the excavated spoil had been spread, I plant some Wild Garlic and Wood Anemones.

Of course, there is much more to do. We still need to sculpt the steep banks of the creek into a gentler slope, so that Newts and other creatures can more easily climb into and out of the water, and to allow water's-edge plants to grow on the slopes. And we need many more ferns on the north bank.

Meanwhile the living world continues about its wild ways. The visiting Heron flies in daily, waiting, watching, to depart with an unlucky frog in his dagger-like beak.

FEBRUARY

It is hungry weather. A **Buzzard** is often about, on the lookout for mice or any small prey that might satisfy his hunger. I observe him for a long time, regally enthroned on his branch. He knows I am here; but so long as I remain perfectly still, he disdains to notice me.

More wild swings in the weather, all through the month. In the first week of February, fierce winter winds bring down dozens of heavy willow branches, a few whole trees. The tangle of broken limbs, toppled crazily one upon another, add to the sense of Amazonian wilderness. I love it! But in places the fallen giants block the paths, or balance precariously above a clearing where children play.

We call on Merlin Harvey, our expert tree-wizard, for

a full day of work with chain saw, ladder, and climbing ropes, to fell and lop the more dangerous limbs. Merlin is a magician. He climbs high into the branches, securely roped to other neighbouring trees. We have a grand day, Merlin, Catherine, and I. In the afternoon the rain comes on again, and by the time we have finished the job we go home soaked. But satisfied, too: job done.

There's another big task ahead. All that tree work has left us with mountains of felled branches and dense tangled brush. We need to lop off the myriad side branches, then saw and stack the bare tree-limbs into compact log piles, to form winter shelters where frogs and newts may hibernate. The densely compacted brush will make equally valuable hiding places for beetles, mice, and countless other small critters.

It will be a lengthy task, all that sawing and lopping and snipping. Over the next few weeks I make a start on it. I take home an armful of the lopped pussy-willow fronds, and stand them in a giant water jug. In the warmth of our kitchen, within a few days the tight silver-grey buds have opened to four times their previous size, stippled in glorious golden pollen.

The weather is mild. We summon another volunteer work party, to do the planting in Railway Wood postponed from the January freeze. Woodland plants: hundreds of Bluebells, Wood Anemones, and Wild Garlic, planted 'in the green', that is, when they have already begun to grow. Our volunteers do a grand job.

SUBURBAN WATER COURSES
The water supply to the Mill Stream has not always been so abundant. Over the years, it gradually slowed to little more

than a trickle, drying up altogether in the summer months.

The water reaches the Trap Grounds by a carefully designed series of swales and ditches, eventually entering the nature reserve from the Waterways housing estate to the north, via the culvert under Frog Lane. Its main source is the outflow from the lake half a mile away, beside Elizabeth Jennings Way. This lake, in turn, is supplied by rainfall across all the surrounding area – runoff from roads and roofs, gardens and driveways – no pristine spring!

Before the water reaches Waterways, it has to cross the Oxford Canal. It does this via a siphon, running *beneath* the canal from east to west. Over several years the siphon had come to function less and less well, becoming increasingly blocked with silt. In 2020, during a period of exceptionally heavy rainfall, the siphon broke. The water came gushing upwards from a hole in the ground, flooding across the towpath before pouring uselessly into the canal, carrying bits of the towpath with it.

All this complex and somewhat precarious watercourse is the responsibility of the privatised Thames Water, with its headquarters on the other side of the world – in Australia. With the tireless support of Adrian Olsen, the Chair of the management company responsible for the Waterways estate, we appealed to Thames Water for urgent repairs, but got no response. We tried various channels to contact them. Then our local Councillor, Tom Landell-Mills, rode to the rescue. Somehow, he obtained the personal email address of the chief executive of Thames Water, and sent him a strongly worded demand, with the threat of legal action. The response was immediate. Within a couple of hours at least four different junior managers were on the job. Forty-eight hours later the siphon was working again – working better than it ever had before.

We now have a steady flow of water into the Mill Stream. It is a pleasure, every time I walk past, to hear it pouring steadily over the little sluice as it leaves the Waterways.

JACK FROST

It is mid-February, and abruptly winter is back. An icy east wind: the tabloids call it 'the Beast from the East'. Snow sparsely covers the frozen ground. The ponds are lined and rimed with ice, growing thicker night after night. Where reeds or branches emerge from the frozen ponds, the ice has formed elaborate patterns around them: concentric rings of light and dark which interweave like contours on a map. I can see the leaves of marsh marigolds and Loddon lilies trapped beneath the ice. Snowdrops, many of which had opened in January, have all shut tight their delicate hanging flowerheads.

For ten days the freeze continues. Rarely the thermometer creeps above zero for an hour or so in the afternoon, to plunge back well below every night. Mornings are misty; hoar frost coats everything. My breath smokes, adding to the mist. Dog walkers appear bundled up like Michelin-men in quilted coats, scarves, fur hats. Even their dogs wear overcoats. Their kids entertain themselves by tossing logs on to the frozen ponds to see how far they will slide. One day, when the ice has all melted, we'll drag them laboriously ashore again.

The ground is rock-hard. Footpaths, which in January were deep in mud, are hard as iron. Ironically, a long-awaited grant from the City Council to pay for more gravel for footpaths has just come in. We purchase five more tons of gravel, and arrange two volunteer work parties, for a

Saturday and Sunday afternoon, to spread it on what had been the muddiest remaining sections of the footpaths. Out of the long Coronavirus lockdown, our Trap Grounds volunteers are like corks out of a bottle. Over the weekend they put in a total of 24 volunteer-hours, trundling heavily laden wheelbarrows, to spread all five tons of gravel along the paths. Coats come off: it is warm work, despite the cold air. Everyone seems to enjoy it, the chance to be outdoors, the companionship, all the while staying carefully spaced out because of the pandemic.

✼ ✼ ✼

Once more, within 24 hours the temperature swings from below freezing to around 10°C. A huge relief for hungry birds as well as humans. Thrushes, Wrens, Robins, Great Tits, silent and unseen for the past ten days, can all be heard singing again. The sky is blue, the sun shines on every twig. Joggers are back along the canal towpath in shorts and T-shirts.

Our pair of swans, Edwina and Prince, have returned. Last year they nested by the canal, raising five healthy cygnets, now full-grown. The adult swans choose a different nest site each year, and now they are prospecting our reedbed for a new home. Through most of January they could be seen, accompanied by their five cygnets, along the canal nearby. But before the end of January one of the cygnets – a male – has been chased away by his parents, to reappear on Port Meadow. A few weeks later the remaining four females have likewise been kicked out to fend for themselves, and sally off to join their brother.

The year before last, 2019, brought a catastrophe for Ethel

and Ernest, the swans then nesting on the Trap Grounds. They had built a fine big nest and begun to lay. All seemed well. Then, half-way through egg laying, the pair of swans abruptly abandoned their nest and fled in panic. One egg was found abandoned in Frog Lane, cold; we found another – smashed and eaten – in another part of the site.

What could have so startled and terrified these magnificent birds? What animal could have such an effect? The answer gradually emerged. We had had occasional sightings of what finally revealed itself as an American Snapping Turtle, an armour-plated amphibian the size of a cauldron-lid, with a long neck and a beak capable of severing a human finger. Such a creature would be unknown to our swans. Its sudden appearance, hissing and snapping, perhaps on the hunt for eggs, could have unnerved them utterly. It's a North American species, living in shallow ponds and streams. In southern England, the only way they come to be living in the wild is through the irresponsible release of unwanted pets. They can survive cold winters, and may live to a great age.

We were in correspondence with a turtle and terrapin enthusiast, Dave Willis, who had already housed 80 rescued terrapins. He told us, never try to pick up a Snapping Turtle! The safe way to capture one is to wrap it in a blanket so it cannot turn its long neck and bite you. Well, eventually our Snapping Turtle was captured, and Dave generously gave it a home. But our beautiful swans had no cygnets that year.

❋ ❋ ❋

All through the last ten days of February the weather continues balmy. The leaf buds on the hazels are swelling;

hazel catkins are powdered in yellow. Shake a branch and a cloud of pollen drifts on the wind. In the woodlands, the dark-leaved Spurge Laurel has opened its densely clustered, yellow-green flowers. It is well worth stooping to inhale their faintly musky scent!

Slowly, cautiously, the plant world is coming back to life. Every year, for several years past, we have lifted and divided big clumps of Snowdrops after flowering, to replant them in smaller clumps so they will spread yet more. This year, Snowdrops throng the Trap Grounds' aptly named Snowdrop Meadow in shining drifts. And close on their heels come the primroses.

In autumn 2020, our volunteers planted a thousand Wild Daffodil bulbs, thanks to a generous gift from a supporter. A thousand dry, papery bulbs. It took several days of work parties to prepare all the planting-holes and get the bulbs planted, four inches down, bedded into soft soil, in clumps of between six and ten. Out came yet more broken bricks and bottles; the planting holes to be back-filled with fresh topsoil. We planted 330 bulbs in Foxglove Meadow, another 330 in School Meadow. A third batch of 330 went in near the entrance to the Trap Grounds, along the muddy bank that the dredger had created out of the piled-up, streaming wet silt from the Frog Lane ditch. When we came to plant the Daffodils there, the silt was still alarmingly wet, even two months after the dredging. I worried that the bulbs might rot in this damp environment.

Now, in the last week of February, after three months of their winter sleep, all those daffodils have reawakened, pushing up vigorously through the damp soil. Pale green spires appear. Within just a few days they have nodding flower buds. I am overwhelmed by my own response to seeing their fresh green shoots: intense relief, mixed with leaping delight. They have survived, they're alive! The marvellous, magical Spring is on its way!

This means there are urgent tasks to complete before *other* plants emerge from dormancy. First, I have a dozen Hart's-tongue ferns to plant out beside the stream. We planted a few there two years ago, and they have thrived; so it's a habitat they are happy in. Hidden in the woodland among the brambles and half-buried bricks, I have a little fern nursery from which each year I harvest a few plants; and where each year new baby ferns appear. But few people are likely to see them there. On the stream bank, beside the boardwalk, scores of people will walk past them every day. So there I am on hands and knees, planting out a dozen of these elegant, evergreen ferns, still with their over-wintered green fronds. In a few weeks' time the ferns will re-awaken and put out their new tightly curled shoots like bishops' crooks.

Another, similar, task is to transplant some of the equally beautiful – but unkindly named – Stinking Hellebores. As with the Hart's-tongue, the hellebores have spread in abundance in one or two hidden-away, shaded corners of the Trap Grounds, where few people ever see them. They are handsome, tufted, early flowering plants, though far less flamboyant than the daffodils. Even their flowers are green, though delicately edged with mauve.

The last weekend of the month, 27th and 28th of February, are days of radiant sunshine. Scarcely a cloud to be seen; the air is soft and warm. Visitors stroll along the boardwalk all day. Birdsong, louder and sweeter than any we have heard this year, fills the woodland. In the evening, the full moon shines high in the sky, lighting the paths, the ponds, the stream, long after sunset.

On 25th February I hear a **Chiff-chaff** warbler singing. The first of the year; he must have overwintered here in England, perhaps right here in the Trap Grounds. Next day he is singing again. His simple little song, *chip, chop, chip, chip, chop…* goes on and on. It lifts my heart. A few days later, another Chiff-chaff is singing in a different part of the site.

MARCH

Eddie and Prince, our handsome pair of **Mute Swans**, have had frequent matings on the pond, preceded each time by an elaborate courtship ritual: alternately dipping their heads in the water, bowing, circling closer and closer, then rising breast to breast, entwining their long necks together.

They have built a bulky nest at the south end of our (appropriately named) Swan Pond. Eddie is sitting, with her head under her wing, while Prince keeps watch at the north end of the pond.

March is notorious as the most changeable of months. After the burst of sunny Spring weather at the end of February, March has returned with a grey overcast. That does not seem to worry the plant world. Blackthorn and Cherry-plum are now starry with delicate white blossom.

The huge Cherry-plum at the entrance to Burgess Field is a magnificent sight: a blossom-covered dome twenty feet high, twenty feet across. How many years will it be before some of our own Spring-flowering trees, planted ten or fifteen years ago, have grown as big?

Today, the 5th of March, they wait patiently under a steady drizzle, every twig, every petal laden with droplets. Brush against them and your arm is soaked. The hawthorns are crowded with bright green leaf buds, still embryonic, still tightly furled, but ready to open with the next sustained burst of warmth.

In the fleeting patches of sunlight, the scattered Cherry-plum bushes suddenly blaze in slender pillars of white blossom and tiny leaf. The jagged outlines of flowering Blackthorn likewise catch fire along their still leafless, spiny branches. Blackthorn is the food plant for caterpillars of the Brown Hairstreak butterfly. Since we planted them, our Blackthorn bushes have nurtured a small population of this comparatively rare, local – and beautiful – butterfly. Finding their eggs – resembling tiny white golf balls no larger than a pinhead, stuck in the crook of a branch – is a subtle skill. Nicola Devine has it to perfection.

Then comes a weekend of clear skies and radiant sunshine. The sun is warm on my back as I kneel to work in the Snowdrop Glade. The snowdrops have now finished their February flowering. I spend several pleasant afternoons dividing the biggest clumps, lifting them from places where few people can see them, to create many new, smaller clumps near the path. Next February their modest blooms may be seen by still more passers-by – and perhaps raise their spirits, as they raise mine.

✸ ✸ ✸

March keeps up its swings. Violent south-westerly winds have returned: wild Atlantic weather, gusting up to 50 miles per hour across Port Meadow. No work on the Trap Grounds for me, today or tomorrow! It may be more sheltered in here than out on the open flood plain, but the branches are still thrashing around like tormented spirits. Overnight, several more willows are down. One of them, laden with golden pussy-willow flowers, has fallen right across Frog Lane. Fortunately, two of us have managed to drag it aside, to await further lopping when the storm has blown itself out.

Three more days, and the wild weather has passed. Catherine appeals to our supporters for primroses and ferns that people can spare from their gardens. The response is magnificent. We assemble two large wheelbarrows piled high with trays and pots of Primroses, plus half a dozen ferns balanced precariously on top. To do the planting we invite a small work party from St Clare's sixth-form college, assembled by Vicky Bullard. We plant out the Primroses in three different places. First, scattered among the Wild Daffodils along Frog Lane, near the entrance from the canal; next, on a rocky mound beside the so-called Primrose Path – granting this little path a better claim to its title; and lastly in Sycamore Glade. It is a delightful task. We work in dappled Spring sunshine with the birds singing around us. Many of the Primroses are already in flower. By the time we have finished, hundreds of little yellow suns are smiling up at us from the mossy ground.

We plant the ferns on the rubble-filled bank beside the 'Creek', near where our slow-moving stream leaves the Trap

Grounds. It reminds me of other plantings six years ago, on the big spoil-bank formed from digging out Heron Pond, where ferns and wild roses now flourish.

Earlier diggings

Back in October 2015, Tim Wray spent four days excavating Heron Pond with his powerful digger. Over the preceding months I had gathered up thousands of broken bricks from far and wide, transporting them in innumerable barrow-loads, to stack them beneath where Tim would eventually spread the spoil from his digging of the pond. Before he was due to come, on top of the bricks I spread out 105 old motor tyres, collected similarly from wherever they had been dumped in the last century, when the Trap Grounds were the local fly-tip.

On top of all this noisesome junk, in October 2015 Tim then spread the thick wet clay that his digger had excavated from the pond. He piled it two or three feet deep: the tyres and bricks are well hidden! A month later, into the still treacherously wet clay, we planted a dozen Dog Roses, and a dozen Blackthorn bushes. Our welly-boots sank in alarmingly as we worked. Finally, round the edge of this huge clay spoil-bank, beneath the wild roses and the Blackthorn, I planted a score of Hart's-tongue ferns.

Annual General Meeting 2021

On Thursday 18 March we hold our AGM, as we have done every March since 2008. Normally it would be in the big hall of St Margaret's Institute, with poster displays, newly printed greeting-cards for sale, a glass or two of wine in the interval. We have followed a simple formula for the programme. First, we report on the year's conservation work and future plans. After that, members of our committee provide a swift round-up of some of the local wildlife, illustrated by Nicola Devine's beautiful photographs. Then, after a break for a glass of wine and a chat, an invited speaker gives us a talk and a slide show on some wildlife topic.

Over the years, we have had a steady turn-out of around 30-40 loyal Trap Grounds supporters. And we have had some wonderful talks. This year, in the pandemic lockdown, our 2021 AGM has to be a virtual gathering, by Zoom, the participants sitting at their home computer-screens. Encouragingly, some 60 people take part. (We have about 275 subscribers altogether.)

This year our invited speaker is Stephen Burch, the Dragonfly Recorder for Oxfordshire, a brilliant photographer of birds and insects. We are treated to exquisite images of the dragonflies and damselflies seen on the Trap Grounds – Stephen's own photos and equally dramatic ones by Nicola Devine. To date, he told us, a total of twenty-two species of *Odonata* has been recorded within our small, ten-acre wildlife site. That amounts to two-thirds of the *Odonata* species ever recorded in the whole of Oxfordshire, including one species never seen in the area before 2020: the Willow Emerald damselfly, which has now begun breeding in the Trap Grounds. Our wetlands are full of life! It is a wonderful payoff for the labour of digging out our six ponds, the dredging of the stream, and their careful maintenance. Stephen is full of praise for Nicola's patient, skilled photographic work, and her self-taught expertise in the matter of *Odonata* identification.

Spring mowing and planting

Early in the year, the more vigorous meadow grasses start

to grow, well before most of the other wildflowers, still locked fast in their winter sleep, no more than tiny leaf-rosettes flat to the ground. At this stage, the vigorous grasses can be cropped back, much as a herd of deer or a flock of sheep might do, leaving the wildflowers untouched. Robert Silverwood knows just how to strim down hard on the coarsest grass, carefully avoiding the clumps of Snowdrops and Primroses.

Indeed, we have found that an early Spring grazing – or rather, mowing – is key to establishing a successful flower meadow. It discourages the tall, lank grasses from dominating. Over time, the balance shifts, the coarse grasses cease to blanket out the slower-growing wildflowers. A flowering meadow begins to flourish.

Last year, by February 2020 the grass had already begun its new growth. We booked Robert for three days of Spring mowing, at weekly intervals, beginning as early as the 6th of March. This year, 2021, the spring regrowth is a full month later, held back by February's 'Beast from the East'. The grass has not put on enough new growth to be worth mowing until the end of March. Robert joined Catherine and me on what became the warmest March day on record, for over a century. As we worked, mowing, and raking the mown grass into small haycocks, we stripped off our winter coats and jerseys. It was so warm in the sunshine, we rested gratefully in the dappled shade to eat our picnics.

To continue the spread of early Spring wildflowers across the meadows, which I long to see, we organise another work party, for the last weekend of March – this time a group of our own Trap Grounds volunteers. Catherine issued a renewed appeal for plants, and once more our supporters contribute a bonanza of Primroses and Celandines. One generous friend, Anne Cowan, gives us a piled-high barrow-load of Primroses. In further preparation for our planting party, I spend a couple of days digging out a hidden treasure-trove of snowdrops from a corner of the woodland, where they have spread profusely in the dark leaf mould, but where – under the trees – they seldom flower. On Sunday, a dozen volunteers set to work, digging planting holes, then on hands and knees dividing and planting snowdrops, primroses, and celandines. Generous, greatly valued labour!

Since last year, we have nearly doubled the Snowdrop cover, especially in Snowdrop Glade. Primroses, too, are more widespread than in previous years; and celandines, once well started, are swiftly patch-forming. Cowslips, too, have done well. I sowed them three years ago in Snowdrop Glade, and already they have spread vigorously. Our strategy for early spring wildflowers is working!

Spring

All through the second half of March, almost imperceptibly, life returns, renews itself day by day. Tiny leaf buds unfurl on the hawthorns. In Snowdrop Glade I revel in the delicate carpet of white violets, hundreds of them, modestly hidden in the grass but, every year, creeping and spreading farther and wider.

Unlike the secretive violets, there is no hiding the wild daffodils. Their proud golden trumpets glow in the sunshine. They make a brave show, wherever we have planted them. But even a thousand is not enough to fill the meadows. Perhaps in twenty, thirty, fifty years from now they will have spread and multiplied to truly carpet the ground.

In the damp woodlands, goat-willows are powdered with a million 'pussy' catkins. From a distance the willow trees

look like pale golden domes. Close to, you realise they are
buzzing with early bees.

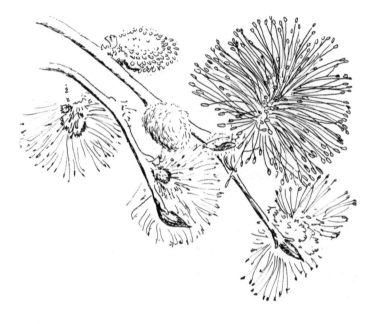

APRIL

April is another month of dramatic changes. At the start of the month, **Primroses** abound; but the trees are still mostly leafless. By mid-way through April the boughs are shimmering in that pale, indescribably tender bloom of new leaf. By the end of the month, almost all the trees except the Oak and Ash are in full green dress.

For three whole months, through March, April, and May, the spring-flowering trees create an unbroken succession of newly opening, blossoming life. First the Cherry-plum, in February, then early in March the Blackthorn flares, whiter than white against its bare, dark-spined twigs, while the gentler Cherry-plum is already in blossom and tiny leaf. By now, in April, the Blackthorn has shed its white petals, although its bushes remain brushed with the cindery grey of a million, million stamens clinging to the flowerheads. Then the Wild Cherry bursts out in its exuberant, hanging clusters of snow.

For two or three weeks the Wild Cherry is queen, before its shining petals, too, float and pile like snowdrifts on the grass. Over the past ten or fifteen years we have planted a score of Wild Cherries: some of them are now three times as tall as me. Beautiful trees! Their shiny reddish bark, banded and ringed, glows in the sunlight; and in early April their long branches are hung with thousands of delicate white flowers.

A few of those we planted – perhaps the shortest saplings – fell victim, however, to hungry Muntjac deer. Muntjac, it seems, have a special fondness for the topmost shoot of a Wild Cherry sapling. No other trees: only the Wild Cherries! Every winter, wherever they could reach them, the deer chewed off the tender growth point. They did it year after year, with the result that those half dozen young trees failed to grow. Five years after we planted them, they were still the same size – or a bit shorter than the day they were planted! The solution was obvious, when I finally got around to it: to fit *two* spiral rabbit guards one above the other around these tiny trees, to protect them above the topmost shoot. Now – at last – those stunted little trees are growing, indeed growing at redoubled speed, their tops already out of reach of even the most agile Muntjac. And this year, for the first time, they have burst into flower, as though saying "thank you!".

Meantime, as the Wild Cherry starts to fade, the delicate Bird Cherry opens its candelabra of sweetly scented white blossoms. Twenty years ago, soon after Swan Pond was created, Catherine and neighbours from Hayfield Road planted a cluster of Bird Cherry saplings beside the pond. Now full-grown. And now, each April, as you enter the Trap Grounds from the canal path you are greeted by their exquisite white fronds. I promise myself: next winter we'll plant some more Bird Cherries.

Towards the end of the month, the apple blossom takes over. There are seven or eight mature apple trees scattered around the Trap Grounds, planted or bird-sown maybe fifty years ago; as well as a dozen Crab Apples that we have planted in the past fifteen years.

All this exuberant outpouring of Spring blossom is the legacy of last year's growth, fuelled by last year's photosynthesis. The energy and nutrients that feed the Spring carnival have been locked inside the trees since the autumn. Through the winter these flower-buds – now opening – were already fully formed, in compact miniature.

Today is the 12th of April. I awake to find the world blanketed in an inch of snow. By 10 a.m. it is already melting, clotting into wet lumps; by noon, except in the shadiest corners, the snow has vanished. The same afternoon I am out in shirtsleeves, gathering up scattered bricks in Cuckoo Copse, my forehead beaded with sweat. We have climate change.

Not so on 18 April 1849, when a great snowstorm engulfed all of Britain. Roads were blocked; coaches were buried in snowdrifts; lambs died within hours of being born.

This year, instead, we have an April drought. Afternoon temperatures regularly reach 15° or 16° C; the soil is dry as dust. I begin to organise a rota of strong-armed helpers to share the task of watering the 200 tender young saplings that we planted last November.

Now, with the warmth and the sunshine come the early butterflies. On mild days, from mid-April onwards, I am seeing half a dozen species about and active: Brimstone,

Comma, Holly Blue, Orange Tip, Peacock, and Speckled Wood. These are all butterflies that hibernate as adults in some sheltered spot through the winter. Then, come any day when the temperature climbs towards 15°C, they are on the wing, looking for nectar, and for a possible mate.

Spring warblers

April is when most of our Spring migrants arrive, some sooner, some later in the month. This year, by the first week of April I hear Blackcap warblers. Soon there are several of them, staking out their territories around the site. And any day now the Garden warblers will be back, too; they seem to particularly favour Railway Wood. The Blackcap is the most virtuoso singer among our regular summer visitors: loud, sweet-toned, with long, inventive sequences of notes. On a good day, the Garden warbler can rival them, but his song has shorter phrases, less liquid than the Blackcap's, with more throaty, guttural sounds.

Around the time when the Blackcaps arrive, just briefly for a day or two there are a couple of Willow Warblers singing. Now, sadly, they have moved on. Twenty years ago Willow Warblers were abundant on the Trap Grounds, chanting their soft, cascading little song from every other willow tree. The song is repeated over and over: the same descending pattern of sweetly whispered notes, a trifle melancholy. But in the early years of the twenty-first century, all over Southern England their numbers plummeted. I last heard a Willow Warbler in the Trap Grounds, singing steadily day after day, maybe ten years ago. How keenly I miss their gentle, confiding company.

But my long-time favourite is the Reed Warbler. Every Spring, I look forward eagerly to the day when I first hear them again, singing in the reedbed. It is usually around mid-April. For me it is one of the marker-points of the year. Not that the Reed Warbler's song is particularly melodious; it is a rather tuneless, scritch-scratch, whirring, churring, chant. But these little birds keep at it, singing from dawn to dusk almost without a break. A few seconds to swallow some gnats – and they are singing again!

Forty or more years ago, the Trap Grounds reedbed was home to a much larger breeding population of Reed Warblers. Just as, forty years ago, Cuckoos could be heard calling here most days. All this was well documented in 1988 in a BBC nature film, presented by David Attenborough. One female Cuckoo was recorded as laying a total of 25 eggs here in one season – a world record, it seems – in 25 different Reed Warblers' nests.

Evidently, in those days our reedbed must have hosted at least 25 breeding pairs of Reed Warbler. No longer! In May 2020 Sam Crofts, a member of our skilled management committee and a professional bird ecologist, made a careful survey of the reedbed, with a colleague, searching for Reed Warbler nests. They found only three nests. In a similar survey the year before, they found just four.

Back then, in the 1980s and 1990s, the Cuckoo's breeding success must have led to a corresponding crash in the local Reed Warbler population. How long it took their numbers to bounce back, if indeed they did, is unknown. In any case, Reed Warblers face other challenges besides the Cuckoo. In 2017, and again in 2020, a pair of Sparrowhawks nested in the Trap Grounds, as they have done in years past. In 2017, they sited their nest right above the boardwalk, giving them a prime outlook across the reedbed – and providing passers-by with the sight of the adult hawks bringing prey to the nest. That season they raised four young hawks. In 2020 they returned, nesting a little way into the aptly named Sparrowhawk Wood, this time fledging three young.

On both occasions, we were treated to a ringside view of **Sparrowhawk flying lessons**. Lessons began out in the open, above the reedbed, the parent-birds calling excitedly, flying wide circuits, urging on their offspring, who trailed awkwardly behind them. Round and round, gathering speed. A short rest-break in the treetops. Then again, excited calling, faster, faster! The circuits tightened; zigzags; figures of eight; jinking and wheeling. In a few days they had progressed to the advanced class – *inside* the woodland – twisting and turning between the crowded willow branches. You could hear the whole family yik-yikking some distance off; then a momentary glimpse as they flashed past overhead. It's a high-risk schooling. Catherine and I counted the cost when we found a young Sparrowhawk sprawled dead on the path, her neck broken.

Keeping all these hungry youngsters fed must have exacted a heavy toll on our small-bird population, on the Reed Warblers perhaps most heavily of all.

WORK PARTIES

Once more, Catherine has appealed for surplus primroses, and once more our generous supporters have provided barrowloads of plants. A group of volunteers has an enjoyable Sunday afternoon planting them out.

We also have need of heavier labour. Wherever we dig – even to plant primroses – up come broken bricks and other debris, dumped on the Trap Grounds throughout much of the 20th century. The twisted metal, broken glass, and suchlike we generally carry off site, to be loaded eventually into a skip and taken to landfill. The dumped bricks and concrete are a different matter. We have hundreds, maybe thousands of tons of them. Over the past 20 years, as we slowly clear the ground, we have gathered up enormous piles of brick rubble here and there around the site.

We decide it is time to cover some of the biggest of these brick-piles with topsoil. We can then plant on top, and, if we are successful, these ugly reminders of the Trap Grounds' past – as an unregulated fly-tip – will be transformed into flowering green hillocks. I am hoping that their fast-draining slopes may be just what some wildflowers, like Marjoram and Bird's-foot Trefoil, like best.

On 24 April a team of twelve from the Oxford Conservation Volunteers, plus four of our own volunteers, assemble for a heavy day's work. This time we have ordered what seems a vast amount of topsoil – eight tons – delivered by hoist in eight one-ton bags over the Navigation Way fence. The biggest task is to shovel the topsoil out of the bags into wheelbarrows, then to trundle these heavy loads to the many brick-piles, scattered in various corners of the site, and finally to spread the topsoil in a deep layer all over them.

To push a fully loaded wheelbarrow up the slope to the top of a big brick pile can take two or even three people. Our volunteers labour magnificently. It is satisfying work. You can clearly see the results: you have altered the local landscape! But we would not ask OCV to do such a heavy and repetitive task all day. There's more fun to be had in skimming duckweed and blanket weed off two of the ponds. Several volunteers don waders, wielding big rakes; two others launch an inflatable kayak; another two, working like Trojans, drag some 50 logs and branches out of Kingfisher Pond, where bored teenagers have tossed them.

Other volunteers have taken a couple of 'tree poppers' to Railway Wood, where a thousand Ash saplings have sprung up, crowding out everything else on the woodland floor. A tree popper is a simple but highly effective device for pulling up young saplings by the roots. It has a clamp that grips the sapling's stem at ground level, and a long lever arm. You pull the lever arm slowly and steadily, and up comes the little tree, roots and all.

Some of the Oak saplings that we planted only a few years ago are already head high. Two volunteers have the task of hammering in six-foot stakes, close beside their trunks, to support the young trees in case of damaging gales. They have a heavy mel with which to hammer in the stakes. One volunteer, wearing a hard hat, holds the stake firm and upright; his colleague climbs a step ladder and drives the stake 40 cm into the ground. Grateful for their strength and skill, I then attach strong ties between stake and tree-trunk. Those young oaks will be safe from gales for the next ten or twenty years of their growing lives.

Yet another pair of volunteers make their way behind the viewing screen on the bank of Tim's Pond, into a thicket of brambles. Over the past year or two, the brambles there have grown so high that you can barely see the pond through the openings in the screen. Our two volunteers set cheerfully to work, to dig out the bramble roots. They have hardly begun, however, when they discover a Long-Tailed Tit's nest, a beautifully woven dome of moss and spiders-webs, attached to the back of the wattle screen. Ten young tits, all crowded together inside the nest, are about to fledge. Now, alarmed by the sudden human incursion they are squeaking excitedly, and one falls out of the nest. A gentle giant picks up the tiny fledgling in his big hands and – as delicately as he can – pops it back into the nest. After that, our volunteers tiptoe quietly away. That bit of bramble bashing will have to wait for another day, when the baby birds have flown.

I am happy to record that, two days later, all ten fledgling **Long-Tailed Tits** were to be seen nearby, scrummed together along one slender branch.

MAY

May 1st. May Morning celebrations in Oxford go back at least 500 years. Traditionally they kick off at 6 a.m., with Magdalen College Choir singing from the top of Magdalen tower to a massed crowd – tens of thousands in recent years – packed together in the High Street below. Morris dancing in Radcliffe Square; impromptu bands; singers; jugglers; breakfasts in the Covered Market. It's all a joyful celebration of Spring.

For the past three decades, our corner of north Oxford

has held its own break-away May Morning celebrations, a gentler, more bucolic version beside the Oxford canal. A garlanded crowd gathers to watch a troop of Morris dancers outside the Anchor pub. In years past, a colossal *papier-mâché* ox would then appear, trundled precariously over the steep canal bridge to join the dancing, a blushing maiden seated on the ox's back.

In recent years, when the Morris dancing is over, the Friends of the Trap Grounds have organised a guided **Bird Song Walk**. Sadly, in 2020 and 2021 the Coronavirus pandemic meant that all these cheerful festivities had to be cancelled. But in May 2021 we contrive at least to offer the Bird Song Walk at 7 am. It is fully booked as soon as advertised. Everyone in a good humour. It's a grey morning, but the birds still oblige with some gorgeous if only slightly dampened song – from Thrush and Blackbird, Robin and Wren, Blackcap and Reed Warbler, Chaffinch and Gold Finch, Great Tit, Blue Tit, Long-tailed Tit; loud *kurruks* from Moorhens; motherly noises from a Mallard mother with a flotilla of ducklings.

The highlight of the walk, however, is the sight of a majestic pair of **Sparrowhawks** high up in a bare Ash tree, in full view from the boardwalk. Around them, the birdsong is noticeably hushed. Then, before our very eyes, the pair of hawks mated, sitting thereafter side by side, their striped breast-feathers all ruffled up, looking immodestly pleased with themselves.

The month of May 2021 turns out to be one of the wettest and coldest for many years. On the 11th we have a dramatic thunderstorm, rumbling and crashing around the purple sky, unleashing day-and-night-long torrents of rain. Water in our six ponds rises to the flood levels of winter. Marsh

Marigolds - now in full golden flower - which had been standing on the dry banks are up to their necks again. And beside the boardwalk the elegant splays of Loddon Lilies, with their exquisite hanging flowerheads, are immersed likewise.

All our flowering plants are late coming into flower this year. Bluebells, Buttercups, Cowslips, Red Campions, Dead-nettles – our common meadow-flowers that are usually flowering by mid-April – are only now beginning to show themselves. For the rest of May, with little sunshine to hurry them on, and few insects around to pollenate them, they continue to bloom in abundance. The Cowslips in Snowdrop Glade – near the back entrance to the Trap Grounds – are a special joy. They seem to thrive here, and have spread over the past few years. Through most of the month they stand proudly above their neighbours, nodding their multiple gold heads in the breeze.

Above and all around the meadows, the May blossom bursts out. No other native tree or shrub is quite as exuberant in its flowering as the Hawthorn, the true May Tree. Soon every Hawthorn is dressed from top to toe in shimmering white. The Trap Grounds are richly endowed with Hawthorns, many full-grown and in their prime. Happily, since they can live to a ripe old age, that endowment may continue to pay its glorious Spring dividend for many future generations.

Not far behind come the Guelder Rose, with their big, showy, Hydrangea-like flower clusters: one of our most handsome native shrubs. Over the past 20 years we have planted two dozen Guelder Rose in sunny spots around the Trap Grounds. Even the youngest of them, only a few years old, are now decked in white blossom.

WILDFLOWER SEEDING

Just before the end of April, some of our biggest brick piles were covered with topsoil by the stalwart Conservation Volunteers. Now, at the beginning of May, I have set aside two or three days to sow their fast-draining slopes with a variety of drought-hardy wildflower seeds: plants like Bird's-foot Trefoil, Herb Robert, Common Toadflax. Sown so late, the seedlings are liable to struggle. Indeed, I worry, will they survive at all? To offset this risk, I also dig up and transplant on to the brick piles several well-grown clumps of Ox-eye Daisies, Forget-me-nots, and Marjoram. And at the base of the mounds, where it will not be so fast-draining, and in the shade, I transplant some vigorous Stinking Hellebores. After a few days of diligent watering, all these transplants look happy in their new homes.

A week before this late-season seed sowing on the brick mounds, I managed to remove two big hay piles, last year's end-of-summer mowings, from the middle of Snowdrop Glade, and to re-site them on the edge of the meadow. By now, any Grass Snakes that might have taken their winter snooze there will be on the move again, so I shall not be disturbing them. Where the hay piles had lain, two round bare patches are left, each about three metres across; and now at last, once I have cleared and gently forked them over, they are ready for seeding. I sow a wide mix of native meadow flowers.

Last year, in Foxglove Meadow, the big earth-mound next to the path was sown with wildflowers in late autumn - a more favourable time of year. But there too, I was way behind schedule. It had taken me much longer than I had imagined to prepare the ground, digging out the coarse grasses, docks, thistles, and nettles that had invaded over the summer. They had already taken deep root on the previously bare mound. By the time I had done all that, and procured the seeds that I wanted, it was October. At long last, with the newly bare soil raked and gently patted down on the steep slopes, I scattered a liberal mixture of annual seeds, including Wild Poppies and Corn Cockle, and a dozen slower-growing perennials. In mid-October the soil was still warm, and within a few weeks the seeds had germinated, pushing up tiny whirls of leaf all over the mound. But by then the air temperatures were dropping, night frosts were beginning, and the growing season was at an end. So that's how my tiny seedlings stayed all through the winter: as frail infants. Anyone climbing or trampling on the steep mound would have done for them. I put up notices, "Wildflower seeding, please keep off". To my relief this request has been totally respected.

For five months the tiny seedlings slept. Not until April this year did they really begin to grow. Now, in May, they are shooting up, two dozen wonderfully varied patterns of leaf and stem, crowded together all over the big mound. I hope that, in June, they will burst into a riot of flowering colours.

But so few insects! Butterflies, which were out and about on warm days in April, now in May are almost nowhere to be seen. The month continues cold and wet. It rains nearly every day. The temperature seldom rises above 15°C, the threshold for most insects to become active and take to the air. Below that temperature they stay dormant and hidden from view.

Work parties
Over the past year, whenever the constraints of Coronavirus lockdowns have permitted, St Clare's Sixth-form College

has brought an enthusiastic young work party to the Trap Grounds, led by Vicky Bullard, a teacher there. St Clare's has a student population drawn from around the world, who come to study for the International Baccalaureate.

On 22 May, Vicky brings seven young students, Chinese, Italian, German, Russian, and English. Today, our main task is to create some inviting paths across the wildflower meadow in Snowdrop Glade, and – as unobtrusively as possible - to fence off the rest. Over the past couple of summers the flowering meadow was criss-crossed by much careless trampling. Once trampled, the plants never stand tall again. The pristine beauty of the meadow is spoiled for everyone else.

My idea is indeed to encourage people to walk right through the meadow, to immerse themselves in its abundance, but to do so via a little network of narrow paths. On either side of the paths, a knee-high fence: a symbolic barrier.

I have already marked out the narrow paths. The first task for the students is to dig up any remaining clumps of wildflowers on those paths, and to re-plant them elsewhere in place of a tussock of coarse grass. We pile the discarded grassy tussocks into a slowly rising ziggurat on the far edge of the meadow.

Armed with loppers, Vicky and five of her volunteers now spread out across the Trap Grounds in search of slender, whippy Hazel wands ten to fifteen feet long. Within half an hour they have gathered more than fifty such wands. We lop off the side shoots, then the slender, topmost section of each wand at a sharp angle, leaving a smooth, uniform rod that can be bent like a bow, with a sharp point at each end.

Finally our little fence can be constructed. We bend each rod into a smooth curve, sticking its two sharpened ends deep into the soft ground, making a strong low hoop, each one overlapping with the next hoop. It looks neat, and our student volunteers are justifiably pleased with their work.

While five students are busy with the fence construction, I engage two of the strongest and most capable, Dmitry and Tommaso, in the challenging task of uprooting three invasive Giant Hogweed plants. Dmitry describes the task: "It involves some risk, because the plant contains a chemical which causes burns. I was working with Tommaso, and we had to cooperate well to dig out all the roots, and to avoid the poison getting on our uncovered skin."

Several students, besides Dmitry, wrote to us afterwards in appreciation. Here's one of them: "I love the environment, and helping the local area brings me great joy. I am glad I can provide a service to the community by improving it for others." And another: "I have learnt the beauty of the surroundings in the nature reserve. I have had a wonderful experience observing the beauty, but also by contributing to it. I feel I am more connected with nature and the environment around me." Music to my ears.

Donald and Suzanne Dalton have re-started their weekly survey of our Slow Worm population. Catherine Robinson and Boyd Roberts began the survey in 2017, and Donald and Suzanne have continued it since then. They lay out two-foot-square black mats, strategically placed around the meadows. On sunny days, these cold-blooded reptiles creep under the black mats to bask in the warmth. But so far, this cold and cloudy May, Slow Worms are scarcely to be seen. They are still underground, awaiting the sunshine.

Wildflowers and weather

Late May, we are nearing the end of the month; it's *still* cold and wet, and the plant world is weeks behind its usual timetable. All the same, a few of our most familiar wildflowers, adapted to cloudy-rainy Britain, put on a brave show.

Cow Parsley is in full flower, and slowly spreading around the meadows, especially where there is partial shade. What a majestic plant the Cow Parsley is, both delicate and architectural! Unregarded because it is so common along our roadsides.

Everyone knows the Meadow Buttercup, perhaps our most abundant wildflower, the tallest and stateliest of the buttercups. It too is spreading across our meadow areas, with its finely cut leaves and shiny gold cups on arching stems. Another of our commonest meadow species is Red Clover, flowering all through from May to September. It spreads in a modest jewelled carpet, half-hidden beneath the tall grasses. You need only stop for a moment and look down to discover it practically everywhere. Its cousin, White Clover, is less tolerant of tall grasses; but wherever the grass is shorter, White Clover spreads its self-rooting stems along the ground to form dense patches of pinkish white. Between them, the clovers help to out-compete the grasses, enabling other wildflowers to thrive.

The keystone of any richly flowering meadow, however, is Yellow Rattle. The roots of Yellow Rattle feed off the grass roots, thereby weakening them, preventing the coarse grasses from dominating and shading out the less vigorous wildflowers. Every year for the past ten years, we have sown Yellow Rattle seed in the Trap Grounds meadows. And this year, 2021, has yielded the best results yet. Wherever there are clumps of Yellow Rattle, you can see the grass is only half as high as elsewhere.

Overhead, the **Apple blossom** has hung on, much later than usual. Every Spring, you can watch a magical transformation. The dark apple boughs are suddenly stippled in tiny pink buds. It's the pink of the sepals, which enclose the still tightly furled white petals. Then, as the buds unfurl, there is an all-too-brief moment of the utmost, delicate beauty: the apple blossom is transfigured into garlands of clustered pink and white. A moment not to be missed! Within a few days the flowers have opened right out, a froth of glorious white on every twig, and the pink has vanished.

JUNE

S uddenly summer weather is here, after one of the coldest, wettest Mays on record. The temperature has shot up to 20°C; next day it's 23°. Sunny blue skies, day after day, not a cloud to be seen. The temperature soars, and with it the pollen count. The flowering grasses have released a mass of the pollen that they had clung on to all through wet and cloudy May.

The wildflowers, too, are exuberant. **Honeysuckle** scents the air, climbing high above my head. Around the ponds and by the stream, the Yellow Flag Iris is in full glory. In the meadows, Buttercups, Red Campion, Yellow Rattle predominate, until a sudden opening of thousands – tens of thousands! – of Ox-eye Daisies swathe the meadows, eclipsing all beneath them. A few days later, red Poppies burst into flame above the newly planted mound in Foxglove Meadow. All at once it's flaming June.

ECO-SYSTEMS, BIODIVERSITY, CLIMATE CHANGE, AND CLIMATE PROTESTS

An eager group of Oxford biology students, with three of their tutors, come to do an all-day 'BioBlitz' on the Trap Grounds. They send us the results. Assisted by their tutors, they identified over 100 insect species, including at least 30 kinds of beetles, 24 species of bees, wasps, and ants. They counted 64 plant species and spotted 18 different birds. No unexpected rarities, but the biodiversity of our small nature reserve looks to be in sound health.

Would that this were true of our English countryside more widely – the most wildlife-depleted land in Europe! Would that it were true of our whole over-exploited but still miraculous planet!

3 June. Health Ministers of the G7 are meeting all this week in Mansfield College in Oxford. Astonishingly, appallingly, while climate change threatens the future health and indeed survival of seven billion humans, this topic does not appear on the Health Ministers' week-long agenda! Apparently, the governments of the rich, Western world are unconcerned.

While the Health Ministers and their entourage assemble at Mansfield College, a crowd of people who are indeed concerned by these issues gathers in Broad Street. A Samba band rocks the air; we hand out leaflets; passers-by stop and listen to impassioned speeches. Global over-heating *can* still be slowed, even turned around; but only if governments take massive, concerted action. *Now.* Before irreversible, run-away global warming renders much of the planet inhospitable to human life.

After the speeches, there is a symbolic Die-in on the steps of the Clarendon Building. Some forty of us lie down quietly, each covered by a white sheet, while half a dozen medics move from one body to the next, inscribing large Cause of Death certificates: deaths from the many terrible and imminent consequences of global heating. It's peaceful for a while, lying under a sheet. Then the Samba band strikes up again…

WATER, AND WATERING

Heading towards mid-summer, Oxfordshire has not a drop of rain. Day after day of cloudless blue skies. Temperatures up to 28° C. Happily, for now the well-established flower meadows of the Trap Grounds need no watering. The densely crowded wildflowers shade each other, they have grown deep roots, and the shaded soil retains its moisture. So – I reassure myself – they can comfortably endure a brief midsummer drought.

Not so my young seedlings on the steep brick mounds, still struggling to grow on their fast-draining, thin layer of topsoil. Four other patches of cleared ground have also been seeded with wildflowers. Those were on the flat, but here too the half-bare soil swiftly dries out under the hot sun. I begin a regime of daily watering of all these fragile seedlings.

The method has evolved over the years. I carry two hefty, 25-litre canisters to the canal bank. Clambering cautiously down the steep bank, keen to avoid an unintended swim, I lower a watering can into the canal and haul it up, brimming full. With practice I can pour from the watering can into the narrow neck of a canister, without spilling. It takes between three and four watering cans to fill a canister. Now, with the full, heavy canisters tilted at the front of the two-wheeled wheelbarrow, tightly capped, the barrow is nicely balanced. All I need do is to pull the loaded barrow behind me along Frog Lane, then along the boardwalk, through the meadows – or round to Railway Wood – to reach one or other of the big brick mounds. Careful, though! If you raise the handles of the wheelbarrow a little too high, the weight suddenly shifts, the barrow tilts uncontrollably and tips the canisters onto the ground. Then it is all I can do to lift them back aboard.

The next problem is to transfer the water from the canisters back into a watering can. I position a large plastic bucket under the end of the wheelbarrow, unscrew the cap of a canister, and – cautiously – tilt the wheelbarrow. A jet of cool water streams out into the bucket. I re-cap the canister. From now on it's simple. Fill the watering can from the bucket, carry the watering can to a brick mound – and water! One big brick mound can take all 50 litres, and still be thirsty. If I'm feeling strong, I do a second round-trip the same day.

WILDFLOWERS

Red Campions throng the northern half of Snowdrop Glade, much more densely than the southern half. That puzzles me. The northern half of the meadow gets the full midday sun when the southern half is in shade. I had thought that Red Campion shunned the midday sun. I was wrong.

Ox-eye Daisies in full bloom cover much of Snowdrop Glade, as well as all the east side of Foxglove Meadow. From a distance they seem to hide all their shorter neighbours, until you look more closely. Suddenly you realise there is a dense understorey of twenty or more other wildflower species, some close to the ground, some already as tall as the Ox-eyes. There are masses of Clovers, both Red and White, Birdsfoot Trefoil, Forget-me-nots, Ground Ivy, Herb Robert, Knapweed, Meadow Vetchling, Selfheal, Yellow Rattle … Indeed, Yellow Rattle is everywhere.

A few taller plant species have also shot up in the last two weeks, high above the Ox-eye Daisies: Great Mullein, Mugwort, Teasel, Ribbed Melilot, St John's Wort, Wild Carrot. In July, when they're all in flower, their tall spires will dominate the scene.

By now we have had nearly three weeks of drought, with daily temperatures up to 28°C. And two weeks of heavy-duty watering! Finally, rain and thunderstorms are forecast for 18 June, coming from the south. Torrential rain arrives, as forecast, continuing over two whole days and two whole nights, on 18th and again on 20th June. The stream and all our ponds are up several pegs. Heron Swamp, which had dried out, is knee-deep again. The drought is thoroughly broken.

DUCKWEED

For Saturday 19 June we scheduled an afternoon work party with students from St Clare's. Happily, the downpour briefly lets up, before returning in bucketsful next day, so the Saturday work party can go ahead. Vicky brings four stalwarts, including again Dmitry from Russia, and Johannes from Bolzano in the Dolomites.

Our main task of the day is to rake the duckweed and pondweed from the surface of Heron Pond, which has become blanketed in the stuff. Two of the students pull on chest-high waders and stagger out into the pond, armed with our biggest rakes. They drag off colossal swathes of pond weed, passing it on to a third volunteer who laboriously spreads it out along the banks. This is to allow small creatures which may have got trapped in the weed to escape back into the water. I turn over kilos of raked weed, picking out dozens of water snails, which I chuck back in the pond. They include elegant, spiral-pointed Mud Snails, juvenile Great Pond Snails, and the flat, translucent discs of Ramshorn Snails.

The task of pond-raking becomes strangely, almost comically frustrating. You clear an area of water several yards across, but then, even as you watch, the weed closes back over it. You rake it clear again, and within a few minutes it looks as though you had never touched it. Rake a third time, and the same thing happens. Our volunteers gallantly soldier on; the pond weed piles up all around the banks. But eventually hilarity breaks out. The work party turns into a water fight, a pond-weed fight. The students are convulsed with laughter, two of them soaked to the skin. Dripping, draped in pond weed, still laughing, we pack up and carry the gear back to the tool-shed. Everyone has had a good afternoon!

Midsummer

Rain continues, on and off, for the rest of June. Some of the tallest wildflowers are laid flat by the downpours. But at least my belated seedlings are well watered. They have begun to grow. No more trundling of water canisters!

In the brief sunny intervals, at last butterflies and day-flying moths are about. Meadow Brown and Gatekeeper butterflies flicker in and out of view. Scarlet Tiger Moths flash their brilliant underwings. Their black-and-yellow caterpillars feed on Comfrey, Nettle, Hemp Agrimony, all of which we have in abundance. Six-spot Burnets display

their iridescent colours on flowerheads, reluctant to fly.
  Deep in the tall grasses, crickets and **grasshoppers** sing.

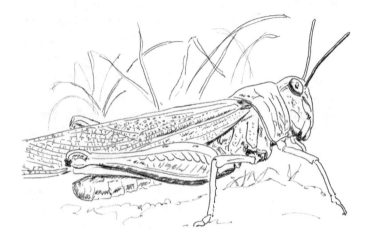

JULY

I sit in the sun. A **Comma butterfly** settles beside me on a sun-warmed stone, opening and closing his wings. After a time he remains still, basking. Like me. Then another Comma flies near, and the two spiral up and up. Eventually, they fly off together, still dancing. No longer singles, they're a pair!

Hoverflies hang in the air, or zip deftly in any direction: backwards, forwards, sideways, down or up. I am in awe of their total command of the air. Their huge compound eyes give them wrap-around vision.

Biodiversity and climate change

In Oxfordshire, early July continues mostly cool and wet. Occasionally, as on Sunday 12 July, the rain is torrential, all day and all night. In contrast, the western USA and British Columbia are suffering furnace-like conditions. Trapped under a vast heat-dome, temperatures have climbed to 49°C, leading to hundreds of heat-related deaths. In Washington State, temperatures are 10°C above any previous records. And with the continuing heat and drought come uncontrollable wildfires, right across the American West. California's wildfire season, which last year was the worst ever known, has again been exceeded. Siberia, too, is in the grip of a searing heatwave and roaring bush fires.

All around the world, climates are changing fast. Scientists believe that the rapid warming in the Arctic over recent decades has slowed the Jet Stream, trapping weather systems. While in Siberia wildfires rage, in Germany and Belgium two months' rainfall hammers down in 48 hours. Hundreds are swept away and drowned, towns and villages devastated. Comparable floods have struck in China, Japan, and other parts of south Asia.

Back here, July should be the peak month for insects. But this year, 2021, through the first half of July there are fewer insects around than any previous year I can remember. I am seeing troublingly few butterflies: some Meadow Browns and Large Whites, a few Ringlets. The other common butterfly species of our flower meadows are scarcely to be seen. Annual surveys by Butterfly Conservation record a 75 per cent drop in butterfly numbers since 1970.

Our cold, wet May, then rain again through the second half of June and into July, has hit the insect world hard – on top of all the other, global challenges of more obviously human origin. Not just the butterflies. The same is true of many other insect families that are normally around and easily seen or heard: bees and bumblebees, grasshoppers, beetles... None seem abundant.

Their scarcity does not stop Nicola Devine, our sharpest-eyed observer of Trap Grounds wildlife, from spotting – and photographing – several rarities. These include a pair of strikingly beautiful Herald moths and a Brimstone moth, not recorded on TG since the 1990s; and a beetle, *Platydracus stercorarius*, with brick-red thorax and striated black-white abdomen, not previously recorded. Congratulations, Nicola!

WORK, AND MORE WORK

On the first Saturday of July we summon a work party, and eight generous volunteers respond. Catherine takes five of them, armed with saws and loppers, to the southern end of the stream, just beyond the small Creek. Here, they set to work on the head-high pile of branches felled by Merlin Harvey last February. In two hours they have reduced the tangle to neatly stacked logs and compact piles of brush. Come next winter, these will provide valuable shelters for hibernating newts, frogs, and other smaller creatures.

Dragging away the felled branches reveals the ugly heap of concrete blocks that has lain there for years. Swapping saws and loppers for spades and shovels, our stalwart volunteers then spread the remaining half ton of topsoil over the concrete rubble.

When we get the next load of topsoil delivered, we can complete the job. Another ton of topsoil should cover it: the rubble will have vanished, in its place a rounded hillock four metres across. We will plant it with ferns and other shade-loving plants. Slowly, slowly, we are transforming this long-neglected and formerly junk-encumbered corner of the Trap Grounds into a place of quiet, secluded beauty.

While all this hard labour with saws, loppers, and shovels is going on, I and three other volunteers are busy planting up two more such topsoil-covered hillocks, each of which conceals piles of broken bricks. First one small mound in School Meadow, then the huge brick mound half-hidden under the giant Sycamore tree to the North of Snowdrop Glade. In April both mounds were covered with topsoil by a dozen strong OCV volunteers. Onto each of these we now transplant big clumps of Marjoram, Hellebores, and Ox-eye Daisies, all thoroughly watered-in. Another two days of watering, and they are looking fine.

Repairing the Boardwalk

The boardwalk, which winds its gentle way alongside the stream, was built with great skill by Stuart Cox from Cambridge, over ten years ago. Before then, there was only a precarious line of stepping-stones by which to traverse the boggiest bits. Not for the faint-hearted: impassable with a child buggy or wheelchair, with many a slip and wet, muddy feet before you reached the farther side.

Back then, I stood by Stuart day by day as he worked, chatting, keeping him company – and guiding the layout: "Let's have a big curve here" … "another one here!"

The boardwalk has transformed visitor access. It remains our biggest and costliest piece of infrastructure, funded by contributions totalling £3,000 from Friends of the Trap Grounds, plus a handsome grant of £20,000 from the Trust for Oxfordshire's Environment. It looks like wood, but is in fact made from re-cycled plastic: far more durable than timber, and non-slip. A happy combination.

However, along one of the softest parts of the streambank, the posts that hold up the boardwalk have slowly, slowly subsided. Over several winters past, whenever the water level was high, this section of the walkway would disappear altogether. You could get by in wellies, if at all.

Now, for three days Stuart is back in Oxford, to raise that section of the boardwalk back up to its original height. It's a skilled operation, requiring a ten-metre-long section of boardwalk to be dismantled, massive new posts driven into the ground, new longitudinal rails fitted, and finally the surface boards reinstated, higher than before. On the way, sure enough, there are hitches. Some boards get broken. But all the while, Stuart remains his cheerful, confident, can-do self.

The recycled plastic planks and posts are imported from Germany. Alas, their supply has been impeded by Brexit and the High-Speed 2 rail project, and prices have skyrocketed. The whole job costs us £1,500. Once it is completed, aside from some shiny new brass screws – and a perfectly level boardwalk – you would scarcely know anything had changed!

THE SPARROWHAWKS ARE BACK

I should have known they'd be back. This year our resident pair of Sparrowhawks has again nested on site. A tribute to the abundance of small birds that make their home here and flourish on the Trap Grounds! Nicola Devine, sharper-eyed than any of us, watched the pair of hawks nest-building in June, gathering twigs to build their bulky nest, then carefully peeling off soft strips of bark to line it. Now, in early July there are three gawky fledgling hawks, small bundles of fluff with over-large heads and huge beaks. Two weeks later they are already long-legged teenagers, clambering on to nearby branches, peering down at us. And barely a week after that, the three youngsters are having their first flying lessons.

A WILDFLOWER WALK

Caroline Jackson-Houlston, an expert naturalist, has offered to lead a wildflower walk around the Trap Grounds. The ten available places are snapped up by TG supporters in no time. We move slowly along the paths, stopping frequently, regaled with countless, fascinating digressions about the many plants we see. It is an education! In the early days, Caroline was an invaluable member of our Trap Grounds committee, expanding our wildlife records, advising on conservation. It is a pleasure to welcome her back.

Several of the meadow areas are approaching their annual peak of floral abundance. And this year, as for several years past, there are some lovely new arrivals.

Two thriving clumps of Restharrow have sprung up thigh-high, lit with a thousand delicate pink pea-flowers. I sowed the seeds two years ago, and this is their first year of flowering. Restharrow spreads by creeping rhizomes. The name refers to their tough, knotted roots, wiry enough to stop a horse-drawn harrow. I am hoping that in years to come they will spread to occupy more of our meadows. I'll try to help them...

The gaudy yellow flowers of Common Toadflax are dotted here and there across the meadow. Short spires of densely packed, snapdragon-like florets, each one with a bright orange lip and long spur. Gorgeous! It's a native English wildflower, despite its exotic air.

We have been less successful with Viper's Bugloss; but at least two isolated plants have come up this year, bearing their column of brilliant blue flowers on a spiny stem. I'm still dreaming of establishing dense patches of Viper's Bugloss in the Trap Grounds meadows, spreading sky-blue pools of summer.

Another handsome species I have been trying to introduce for some years has appeared this year in profusion.

Tall, wiry spires of Chicory, with their sky-blue, rosette-like flowers opening progressively up the stem, now decorate the northern half of Snowdrop Glade, scattered among the equally statuesque, silvery-green Mugwort, and the taller still, yellow-flowered candelabras of Great Mullein. Together, they make a striking architectural contrast. With so much rain in May and later June, plant growth has been exuberant. The Chicory, often little more than waist-high, here arches over my head.

INVADERS

Plants spread in many ways, often by birds distributing their seeds – or seeds blown in the wind – and via creeping roots. And by human introductions. One of the most invasive of non-native plants, the Indian or **Himalayan Balsam**, was introduced to English gardens in 1839. Like other Balsams, it has evolved an exploding seed capsule, which can propel the ripe seeds up to 7 metres in any direction. The plant likes to grow in or near water, and its corky seeds float, to spread swiftly along watercourses, as it has now done over much of England and Wales. Undeniably handsome, with large pinkish-purple flowers (aka 'Policeman's Helmet') and tall, arching, reddish stems, it is nevertheless a colonial bully, out-competing and displacing other waterside flowers.

For this reason, Himalayan Balsam has become a serious threat to our native biodiversity, a "conservationists' nightmare" according to the local Wildlife Trust. Some years ago we found it had appeared in Hook Meadow, the SSSI water-meadow just half a mile north of the Trap Grounds. Hook Meadow is owned by St Edward's School – though sadly neglected. Catherine Robinson appealed urgently to the school authorities to eradicate the plant before it could spread into the neighbouring Waterways estate and thence into the Trap Grounds. But the school took no action. So, for the past three years she and Adrian Olsen, the Chair of the Waterways Management Company, have organised 'Balsam bashing' work parties, summoning volunteers to pull up every one of these invaders before they can disperse their seeds yet further.

Finally, in July 2021, after yet more urging by Catherine and a threat to report them to Natural England, the school summoned members of its own staff to do the job. Thirty individuals waged an all-day war on the rampaging invader. Despite this, a week later, a group of eight volunteers led by Catherine and Adrian still found a lot lurking among the brambles and nettles, and yanked them out too.

Sadly, more Himalayan Balsam seedlings are bound to appear, and yet more of our volunteer work parties will be needed in August, September, even in October.

HEATWAVE

Abruptly, in mid-July, the season swings again from cool and damp to scorching hot. For ten days there is not a cloud; by midday the temperature has climbed to near 30°C. And at last insect numbers are beginning to recover. The meadows are a-buzz. Wildflowers are blooming in ever richer profusion.

I sit in the sun, on the big pile of rocks in the middle of Snowdrop Glade, almost hidden from passers-by by the mass of tall flowering plants which softly perfume the air.

I become still. I become a part of this living abundance. I watch and listen to the grasshoppers, the foraging bumblebees in the flowerheads, the tiny black ants busy around their nest. Beside me, a gorgeous yellow-and-black **Longhorn Beetle**, *Strangalia maculata*, probes the flowerheads with his immensely long, sensitive antennae. Like me, he is half asleep in the sunshine.

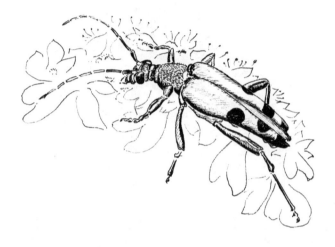

AUGUST

Early August is still high summer. I find a **Grass Snake**, elegantly coiled, basking in the warm sunshine. Wildflowers bloom in profusion; insects forage for nectar, skip and buzz.

By the end of the month it will be autumn, season of fruits and berries, hazelnuts and turning leaves; but for now, it is still the insects' high noon. In the flower meadows there is a constant coming and going of small, winged creatures. In August, the Marjoram is a special favourite of the butterflies; on sunny days it's well worth keeping your eye on their reddish-purple flowers. You may see Small Skippers, Gatekeepers, Meadow Browns, Speckled Woods, an occasional Small Tortoiseshell; as well as several day-flying moths: the Six-spot Burnets with scarlet underwings; one of the beautiful pyralid moths, *Pyrausta aurata*; sometimes a Fiery Clearwing. Always something of interest. Just stand still for a while, and watch.

Hoverflies, too, are active both in the meadows and along the Bramble Path. They include some of our most elegant insects, such as *Helophilus pendulus* with four brilliant yellow stripes on his shiny black thorax. All of them have a breathtaking command of flight, up, down, sideways, backwards, as well as the ability to hang motionless in the air. If you stand perfectly still and raise one forefinger, often a hoverfly will settle on your fingertip, so that you can admire its striking patterns on thorax and abdomen, the beautifully veined, translucent wings that enable its aerial mastery.

Among the grasses, crickets and grasshoppers chirr and wheeze. Disturbed, they can skip twenty or thirty times their own length on their amazing, spring-triggered hindlegs. Lucky for them, as they are a favourite lunch snack for small birds and hungry reptiles.

I have been away with my family in Pembrokeshire, not far from St David's. We go kayaking along the wild north coast, into caves that open into further, dimly blue-lit arches that lead eventually out again to the dancing sea. Compass Jellyfish float gracefully around us. We watch big, powerful Dolphins leaping, leaping.

Out to sea on a bucking inflatable rib, past Ramsey Island, towards evening we find ourselves among hundreds upon hundreds of long-winged Manx Shearwaters, skimming the waves, so close to us that we can almost touch them. It's their regular evening flight home, hundreds of miles from their fishing grounds off the Western Isles, back to their nest burrows on Skomer and Skokholm Islands.

All this makes a dramatic contrast to the more homely,

landlocked wildlife of the Trap Grounds, about as far from the ocean as it is possible to be on this small island. Here the wildlife is more modest in size – you may need a hand lens to fully appreciate some of it – but when you pay it due attention, it's every bit as diverse and wonderful!

❋ ❋ ❋

It is the season for surveys. Catherine and I make an informal survey of the wildflowers in Snowdrop Glade. We count a total of 77 species in that small area. Every year they become more exuberant, and more diverse. No great rarities: most are relatively common. But together they make my heart sing.

Donald and Suzanne Dalton continue their weekly survey of reptiles on the Trap Grounds. They have distributed forty black mats around the site, beneath which the reptiles come to bask and warm themselves. Lifting a mat, it is a wonderful sight to find a family group of full-grown, adolescent, and juvenile Slow Worms dozing, entangled together. If you lift the mat gently, and promptly replace it, they do not stir.

Earlier in the season, reptile numbers were down: not surprising in a mostly cool and wet summer. Now, in August, their numbers have picked up, with a rising count of Slow Worms: some 80 sightings of adults, 30 juveniles. Occasionally, a big Grass Snake, curled up companionably among them.

The mostly cool, wet summer has not favoured dragonflies and damselflies. Nicola Devine reports a marked drop in their numbers this year. There are a few Southern Hawkers about, large gaudy dragonflies, bejewelled in bright green and blue, coasting low down, darting into every little cranny. On occasion they swoop close past me, hawking midges.

Late in the dusk, I sometimes see them, phantom-like, still patrolling their territory.

For the record, here is an alphabetical listing of wildflowers we found in Snowdrop Glade:

Common or Abundant: Bird's-foot Trefoil, Black Horehound, Broad-leaved Dock, Caper Spurge, Chicory, Common Comfrey (with creamy-white flowers), Common Knapweed (including 'an uncommon variant with long, deeply-cut outer florets', *Harrap*), Common Nettle, Common Poppy, Common Ragwort, Common Toadflax, Common Vetch, Corncockle, Cow Parsley, Dandelion, Dove's-foot Crane's-bill, Garlic Mustard, Goat's Beard, Greater Birds-foot Trefoil, Great Mullein, Great Willowherb, Groundsel, Hedge Bedstraw, Hedge Bindweed (alas!), Hedge Woundwort, Herb Robert, Hoary Plantain, Hogweed, Lemon Balm, Marjoram, Meadow Buttercup, Meadow Vetchling, Mugwort (*Artemisia vulgaris*), Musk Mallow, Nipplewort, Ox-eye Daisy, Oxford Ragwort, Red Bartsia, Red Campion, Red Clover, Ribbed Melilot, Ribwort Plantain, Russian Comfrey (pink/purple flowers), Sainfoin, Selfheal, Scentless Mayweed, St John's-wort (both Perforate and Imperforate), Spiny Restharrow, Sun Spurge, Tansy, Tufted Vetch, Weld, White Clover, White Deadnettle, Wild Carrot, Wild Teasel, Wood Avens, Wood Forget-me-not, Yarrow, Yellow Rattle ... [N = 62]

Plus a few scattered specimens that I hope we can spread: Field Scabious, Meadow Crane's-bill, Nettle-leaved Bellflower, Viper's-Bugloss... [66]

And Spring-flowering: Abraham Isaac & Jacob, Cowslip, Dog's Mercury, Germander Speedwell, Ground Ivy, Lesser Celandine, Primrose, Stinking Hellebore, Sweet Violet (White form), Wild Daffodil [N = 11]

With these additions, it comes to a **total of 77 species,** just within Snowdrop Glade. I don't doubt we shall soon find more.

On the 19th of August, Nicola photographed an Elephant Hawk-Moth caterpillar, plump and neatly banded, as big as your thumb. Huge eye-markings on its head, to scare off predators. They feed on Rose Bay Willowherb and Bedstraws – of which we have plenty. The adult moth is an elegant swept-wing wonder with pink and mauve stripes on an olive-green ground.

Tree Plantings

I check up regularly on the young trees that we have planted, particularly the youngest saplings planted only last December. Last year, we planted forty Hazel saplings in Railway Wood, on either side of the path, bare little whips only 50 cm high, plus ten small Hollies. The aim here is to thicken up the woodland understorey, eventually creating a good, dense cover for nesting birds, and for the deer and other wildlife to carry on their woodland lives unseen and undisturbed. It will take a while. Now, in their first year of growth these infant trees still look quite puny.

Our experience is that, after the shock of transplanting, Hazel saplings commonly take a year or two to settle in and spread their roots, before they start to put on height. From then on, however, the young Hazels shoot up. Where they are happy, they can grow up to three feet in a year; in two or three years they can be head high. Another few years and they will have bushed out wide and stand twelve feet tall, providing dense cover. Mission accomplished.

This year, with ample rain – despite two brief dry spells – they appear to be settling in well. So, too, the screening hedge that we also planted last winter in Cuckoo Copse, composed of a hundred baby trees and shrubs, in two close-packed rows. Half of them are shrubs: Wild Privet,

Hedge Honeysuckle, and Blackthorn; the rest are low-growing trees: Hawthorn, Hazel, and Holly. As yet they are barely knee high; but in a few years they will form a dense thicket, a hidden transit route for small creatures as well as a welcome food source for them in the autumn. And, as a bonus, the thicket will hide the railway fence from view along the Bramble Path, and baffle some of the rumble and screech of passing goods trains. The Trap Grounds will gain a little more seclusion from the noisy world around.

My survey of our young trees continues around the site. In Periwinkle Wood there are three dense clusters of Hazels, planted variously over the past three to seven years, and all growing vigorously. Some are still at an early stage, waist high, while others are already arching above my head. Clearly, they are happy to be the under-storey, beneath a shading canopy of much taller Sycamore, Ash, and Chestnut trees. Scattered among the Hazels we have also planted a dozen Hollies, and – mostly deeper into the wood – several slow-growing Yews. Like the Hollies, in time they will form an evergreen screen inside the woodland, further enclosing the Trap Grounds and providing yet more shelter for our ever-growing wildlife. I like to think of those Yew trees, hundreds of years from now. Will they still be there, giant veterans with hollowed trunks, offering their protection to owls and foxes, jays, and woodpeckers? I hope so.

I keep an especially watchful eye on the thirty-plus young Oak trees we have planted - the most majestic of all our native trees. By now some are twenty years old and already three times my height. So far, they appear to be thriving, even though, in winter, the water table can be not far beneath them. Our planting of Oaks has continued year by year. We now have Oaks growing in many parts of the site. Some of the youngest ones were planted to form a sheltering arc to the north and east of Snowdrop Glade. Like the Yews, I wonder, will some of these Oaks still be here, two or three hundred years from now?

❋ ❋ ❋

Around the ponds, shimmering Damselflies float on invisible wings; then settle, allowing me - if I move slowly enough - to approach within inches of them, for a photograph. This one is the **Common Bluetail**, well-named *Ishnura elegans*.

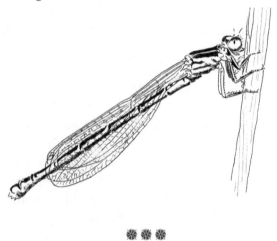

❋ ❋ ❋

Towards the end of August there are signs of autumn on the way, with its many fruits: a precious supply for birds and others, including humans. First off are the Blackberries. It is a magnificent year for them. I have picked basketsful of sweet, juicy Blackberries, to make gallons of Blackberry coulis, the pips sieved off, to be stored in the freezer and used through the winter.

Apples are ripening too, and beginning to fall, although the Crab Apples hold on to their fruit a while yet. Even more favoured by Redwings are the haws, which now hang from countless Hawthorn branches in heavy red bunches. Rose hips crowd the arching stems of Dog Rose. Here and there, too, are swags of Elderberries in lush, juicy purple.

SEPTEMBER

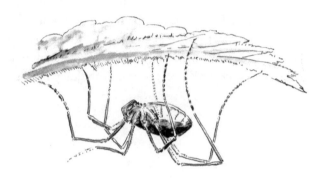

I love the countless smaller inhabitants of the Trap Grounds – the mini-beasts. This is one of the **Harvestmen**, *Mitopus morio*. Like spiders, Harvestmen have eight legs; but they do not spin silk. They hunt mostly at night, catching small invertebrates. When chased by another predator they can shed a leg, which continues to kick, distracting their pursuer. This chap is dozing under a leaf, awaiting the night-time.

September has heralded the return of balmy weather: an 'Indian Summer'. Days of full, strong sun and cloudless blue, interleaved with occasional overcast days, but continuing mild and mellow. The rich colours of autumn – reds, browns, and golds – are slowly building. The Virginia Creeper, which has ramped over some of the trees between Slow-worm Glade and the railway, is already clothed in scarlet. It dangles from the branches in long fiery streamers.

The Rowans are festooned with clusters of red berries. Spindle bushes, slender and fragile looking, seldom more than eight feet high, have begun their autumn display of shocking pink berries, opening to expose the bright orange seeds inside. And soon their pointed leaves will be suffused with scarlet. The Spindle's hard, pale wood belies its fragile looks. It was traditionally used for skewers, toothpicks, and knitting needles, as well as for the weighted spindle used to spin raw wool.

Less ostentatious, the Dogwood berries, half hidden beneath their broad, ribbed leaves, are turning from green to purple. Soon those leaves too will be tinged with claret. Beside them, boldest of all, the Guelder Roses catch fire, with swags of berries of intense, glossy, waxy red.

On 2 September, Carl Whitehead brings his nine Council volunteers to scythe this year's block of the Reed Bed. Their skill with the Austrian scythes is impressive. The sharp blades swish, swish, in unhasting rhythm; the scythed reeds collapse in purple-plumed drifts, to be raked up and pitch-forked into bulky stacks, two metres high and four across. It's a timeless, bucolic scene.

This September, as for the past four or five years, they do a magnificent job for us, cutting and raking a 400-square-metre block of reeds, then piling the cut reeds into three or four tall, compact ricks. The aim of all this is to prevent the past years' dead reeds from piling up year by year on the reedbed floor, raising its level such that the reedbed eventually dries out. If it did, it would swiftly revert to willow scrub and finally woodland. In perhaps 15 years these wonderful volunteers will have worked their way all around the reedbed, ready to start again.

On the 3rd of September, Nicola photographs several pairs of the rare and beautiful Willow Emerald damselfly, *Chalcolestes viridis*, mating and egg-laying around Swan Pond. These delicate beauties continue busily through the month. This is only the second year they have bred here.

Indeed, until three years ago this species had not been seen in Oxfordshire. Year by year they are rapidly spreading northwards from the south coast: one more index of a warming climate.

Sharp-eyed as ever, Nicola also records occasional sightings of the elusive Brown Hairstreak butterfly, egg-laying on the Blackthorn bushes. This beautiful butterfly spends most of its life out of sight in the tree canopy, where it feeds on honeydew. The males congregate high up in a favoured Ash tree, the 'master tree', to await the females, and only rarely descend. But on warm sunny days, the females come down to lay their eggs. Just now, the second week of September, we have five days of uninterrupted sunshine.

The sun has likewise brought out the spectacular Silver-washed Fritillary, twisting and gliding powerfully across the glades. Its bright orange and black-streaked upper wings flash in the sunlight. When it settles, you can see the delicate silver markings on the pale green underwing.

The caterpillar of this wonderful insect feeds on the leaves of wild Violets. But in August, when egg-laying occurs, the Violet leaves have died back and are nowhere to be seen – at least, by me. The adult females lay their eggs on the creviced trunk of an Oak tree, beneath which Violets grow. In the spring, the tiny caterpillars must climb down – often from high up on the tree trunk – to find their food plant. I ask myself: in late summer, how does the butterfly detect the presence of Violets? So much we have yet to discover about the complex behaviours of our local wildlife!

In the Trap Grounds we have a luxuriant patch of wild Violets in Snowdrop Glade. I have planted an Oak tree, now twelve years old, directly above this precious patch. How long will it be before the trunk is sufficiently fissured with age, and this gorgeous butterfly decides to lay her eggs there?

MOWING THE MEADOWS

Many years ago I asked our local Wildlife Trust if we might borrow a few of their Jacob sheep to graze our meadow areas. No, they told me, regretfully, the broken glass and other debris, from the days when the Trap Grounds was a fly-tip, make this too hazardous for the animals. Instead, every year at the end of summer we must somehow mow the grass ourselves.

For several years, the City Council's Countryside service brought a giant mower, with Gary to drive it, and cut it for us. Then, for a few years we did the job ourselves, with Austrian scythes. It made a picturesque, Tolstoyan scene, our shirt-sleeved volunteers scattered across the meadow, earnestly scything and raking the mown grass. Every 15 minutes or so you must stop to re-sharpen your scythe.

In 2014 the BBC's Countryfile team made a film of us toiling in the sun, which was shown on BBC2. After we had finished mowing the largest meadow area, and piled the hay into two or three tall haycocks, the BBC film-crew decided that some of their previous 'takes' weren't good enough. They wanted us to dismantle the haycocks and pretend to mow the meadow all over again. We obliged, as best we could.

Wielding a scythe can be pleasant enough for an hour or so, but it is hard and thirsty work; and most of us lacked the skill needed. I certainly did! Sometimes all I seemed to do with my scythe blade was momentarily to flatten the long grass, which sprang back up after the scythe had passed.

After a few years, we prudently gave away our Austrian scythes to the City Council's countryside volunteers, on condition that they now come, once a year, to scythe a section of our reed bed. It has been an excellent bargain. Their group includes some highly skilled scythe handlers.

As for the meadows, since the days when we attempted to scythe them ourselves, Robert Silverwood has taken over this task. He does it with great skill, with a heavy-duty strimmer. At the end of summer, when the wildflowers have set their seeds, we pay Robert to do a full five days' mowing for us. We leave the mown hay to lie for a few days, to allow the flower seeds to drop; then Catherine rallies a group of volunteers to rake the mowings into tall haycocks. These become a favoured hibernation site for grass snakes. If we get it right, the composting process will keep the grass-heap warm all winter.

❋ ❋ ❋

Mid-September continues warm and dry, except – frustratingly – the very day that Robert Silverwood is scheduled to begin mowing the meadows. Torrential rain falls all this morning. By the afternoon Robert can do some strimming, but barely a third of what we had planned.

Soon, however, sunny days return. By the weekend, skies are cloudless again and the temperature soars. Catherine and I welcome the first work party of the new school year: eight students, four boys and four girls, from St Clare's Sixth-Form College. Some are old hands, like Dmitry, returning for their final year; the old hands give the newcomers to the Trap Grounds an enthusiastic guided tour.

Their first task is to rake the mown meadow grass into tall haycocks. All eight students are hard at work. As they rake, the stubble is hopping with scores of frogs, miraculously unscathed by Robert's strimmer a few days earlier. When that job is done, I lead the four young lads on a squishy trek through the Willow carr and into the reed bed, where the block of reeds was scythed two weeks ago. The boys put in another hour of strenuous raking, adding to the already head-high stacks of cut reeds. It is sweaty work under the hot afternoon sun. On all four sides we are enclosed by swishing reeds, standing eight foot high; we have a pleasant feeling of being hidden from the world in this secret place.

Days of warm sunshine and cloudless nights continue almost to the end of September. The Harvest moon is full. It rises behind the willows along the canal path, huge and luminous, lighting up the reed bed, the stream, the meadows in a golden glow. Two days later is the Autumnal Equinox.

Robert returns for his second day's mowing. He can give us just one day's work each week, for the five weeks that it will take. I accompany him through the morning; Catherine and four volunteers join us for the afternoon's raking. Robert skilfully leaves little islands uncut where the feathery *Artemisia* and other flowering plants have yet to drop their seeds. Today it is sunny and warm. He is able to cover a lot more ground, including most of School Meadow and the southern part of Foxglove Meadow. It's a dramatic transformation, from swishing, knee-high vegetation to a short-cropped, tussocky sward. By the end of the day's raking, the meadows are dotted with tall haycocks, sited in sunny spots for reptiles and others to hide in through the winter.

Through most of this sunny September, many plants continue to flower profusely, like the Common Toadflax, Restharrow and Marjoram. The statuesque Mullein and Wild Chicory are likewise still flowering, as is the St John's-wort; and here and there the mauve flower-heads of Field Scabious continue to float above the grasses. To allow all these precious flowering plants to set seed, we postpone mowing the most flower-rich areas until October.

❋ ❋ ❋

September is also the season of bramble imperialism. Over just a few weeks they produce astonishingly fast-growing shoots, up to four or five metres long. The farthest tip pushes into the ground, sprouting little white roots. Next year, the plant can leapfrog another five metres from there. So, if you leave them to grow, in a few years you'll have no open meadow left, just an impenetrable bramble thicket.

Some bramble shoots arch high overhead: you can't miss them; others snake half-hidden through the grass. If you pull steadily, with a well-gloved hand, an immensely long stem is slowly disentangled from beneath the tussocks. Do this before the end of September, and the cluster of new white roots comes out easily with it, still attached to the end. Later, into October or November, and you'll have to dig them out with a fork or a mattock.

All through September I engage in solo, bramble-uprooting sessions. The borders of every meadow area have been thickly invaded. The northern border of Snowdrop Glade, and the southeast quarter of Foxglove Meadow are the most challenging; but brambles invade everywhere. When I run out of time, or my back complains too much, I just lop the brambles to ground level. It's a less effective, short-term solution, but not so hard on the back!

❋ ❋ ❋

We have reached the last four days of the month, and the long Indian Summer is suddenly at an end. The temperature drops overnight from near 20 to around 10 degrees C. And with it comes the rain.

Happily, on the 28th of September the rain eases off enough to permit Robert to complete his third day of mowing. Occasional showers do not deter him. The tall vegetation near the back entrance is strimmed and raked, as well as the outer edges of Snowdrop Glade. Then Robert moves to Slowworm Glade, where he works on determinedly until it has been laid flat. Ahead of him, to make the mowing easier, Catherine and I have lopped a mass of brambles, now piled waist-high beneath the neighbouring branches.

Over the next two days, 29th and 30th September, the rain comes down again in torrents. A bowl that I have left outside is filled four inches deep. It is a much-needed watering, after four weeks with almost none!

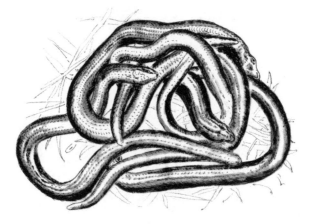

The year is turning. Suzanne and Donald have now completed their week-by-week survey of **Slow-worms** – our legless lizards – for the 2021 season, carefully recording the numbers that they find basking under each of nearly 40 black mats. This year, mats were laid for the first time in two of the Trap Grounds' most flower-rich areas – in Snowdrop Glade and on the east side of Dragonfly Pool – where they attracted good numbers of Slow-worms, plus the occasional Grass-snake. The Sycamore Glade was the best endowed area, with a total of over 200 Slow-worm sightings this season.

Overall, despite a late start owing to the cold, wet month of May, the total number of Slow-worms recorded by Suzanne and Donald in 2021 shows a 25 per cent increase, compared with the previous year. Grass-snake numbers are up, too. Our reptile population appears to be in excellent health.

OCTOBER

From underground, the fruiting bodies of countless species of fungi burst out in lavish display. Some are small and delicate, like the **Fairy Inkcaps** sketched above. Some are brightly multi-coloured, like the fans of Turkeytail fungus; some glowing red, like the Scarlet Elf Cups; while others emerge from rotting tree-stumps in gnarled slabs, orange, mauve, and white.

The autumn is building in lush profusion. Beside the little **Creek,** where early this year we planted two dozen straggly ferns on the bare, inhospitable-looking banks, there is now a jungle of gracefully inter-arching fronds. The ferns have grown and flourished in the frequent downpours. Beneath them, some small animal has dug a couple of tunnels deep into the bank. I wonder who it can be. Perhaps the weasel that Nicola has occasionally caught on camera?

The kingfishers are around. They can be seen most days on a perch overlooking Swan Pond. A sudden dive, a splash, and back with a minnow in its beak.

October is a busy month for the Friends of the Trap Grounds. For one thing, it is the prime season for planting Spring-flowering bulbs. I have purchased 250 rhizomes of the exquisite Wood Anemone, plus 100 more Bluebell bulbs. We'll plant them in small clumps beside the paths, in the semi-shade that they like. If the flowers are happy where they are, as I hope, they will gradually spread. In ten or twenty years' time, will they carpet the ground?

In preparation for planting these and other precious plants, we order three tons of topsoil, to be delivered in three huge bags, hoisted over the Navigation Way fence.

The next step is to dig out the planting holes. To plant seven or eight bulbs per clump, we'll need around fifty planting holes: each hole at least 20 cm wide and 20 cm deep. That's a lot of holes; and a lot of hard digging with mattocks, given the rubble-strewn nature of the Trap Grounds! We call on the services of our skilled and stalwart friends, the Oxford Conservation Volunteers. And, as always, they do a grand job for us! Not only fifty planting holes, neatly dug, but topsoil loaded into groaning wheelbarrows and distributed, in 20-odd piles, adjacent to the planting sites. Next day, I gather up all the rubble they have unearthed. It fills two barrow loads!

A week later, we welcome a robust and cheerful group of students from St Clare's College to plant out all 350 bulbs. It calls for careful work; each student has a page with my rough drawings to guide them. First, at the bottom of each planting hole they place a good layer of topsoil, with more topsoil patted firmly around the sides; then, very gently, they press the seven or eight bulbs or rhizomes into place, in a small circle - making sure the Wood Anemones' slender rhizomes are the right way up; now they cover them with more topsoil, pressed firmly down, and then back-fill to ground level. Job done.

Last week, while the Conservation Volunteers were excavating all those planting holes, Phil Hunter pulled on waders, to stand thigh-deep in Dragonfly Pool, where reeds have invaded one side. He works steadily, digging out their roots and deepening the Pool, while a colleague gathers the voluminous, dripping roots and spoil into a six-foot-high ziggurat above the bank.

The Water Lily, which Catherine planted in Dragonfly Pool ten years ago, has thrived; but it has now grown too big for the location – filling one end of the pond. So, still in waders, Phil turns to dividing its roots. He leaves half the Lily roots intact, excavating the other half to make three or four big new clumps.

A few days later, Catherine and I plant these out into other ponds, including one clump of Lily roots in Swan Pond and one in the Mill Stream. It's not an easy task. Lily roots are naturally buoyant: they float up to the surface if not firmly embedded. To anchor them to the bed of pond or stream, we cram the roots into wicker baskets, which we weight down with large stones to prevent them – absurdly – simply floating away. It works!

Mowing of the meadows continues week by week. On the first occasion this month, Robert and I are accompanied by Marion, my niece from Edinburgh, down South for a week. She and I gather up armfuls of mown wildflowers from the East bank of Dragonfly Pool, and strew them on nearby less flower-rich areas, to drop their seeds.

Mid-October, and Robert comes for a final, long day's mowing, first in the florally-rich Snowdrop Glade, and then – working very fast – beside the railway in Cuckoo Copse.

Catherine accompanies him all day long. Next morning I rake barrowloads of cut wildflowers from Snowdrop Glade, and spread them all over School Meadow. Their seeds will fall and – with luck - germinate there, distributing ever more flowering plants where grass previously dominated.

Back in September I collected a variety of seeds from Snowdrop Glade – Red Campion, Field Scabious, Wild Carrot and suchlike. Now at last, with the meadows mown, it's time to sow them. I dig up grassy tussocks here and there in the meadows, and rake hard to create patches of bare soil. (That's the hard bit.) Now I can sprinkle the precious seeds in those bare patches, and gently press them in.

Autumn magic

Through the second half of October, the magical transformations of autumn swirl and flare across the Trap Grounds. In the soft wind, young Birch trees shimmer lemon and lime. Slowly the lemon turns to gold. Already, there are drifts of tiny gold leaf underfoot. Dogwood leaves, dark green all summer, are now ochre, translucent, their tips suffused in burgundy.

Where Wild Clematis has scrambled over the Dog Rose bushes, thousands of rose hips thrust their red tips from among the curly froth of Old Man's Beard. Hawthorn leaves slowly turn pale, then yellow, then fall, exposing ever more boldly the millions of dark red Haws that crowd every gnarled twig. Spiders' webs, outlined in dewdrops, hang between them.

Towards the end of the month, both the Guelder Rose and Spindle bushes embark on their long blaze of glory. The narrow Spindle leaves have turned cream, gold, pink, scarlet, in a delicate kaleidoscope of colour. The Guelder Rose, more brazenly, mixes many colours within a single leaf: each vein outlined in pale yellow, melting into speckled green and gold, while the leaf edges are bold vermillion. But every leaf is different! And among these lurid leaves hang their shiny, shocking-red berries in heavy bunches.

Amazingly, in the last few days of October some of the Wild Chicory spires still carry freshly opened, sky-blue flowers. And beside them, bright yellow flowers still cling to the Great Mullein.

In the twilight, a **Muntjac deer** emerges silently from among these tall, statuesque stems. We gaze at one another for a long moment, without moving. Not even blinking. Then he shakes his head, turns, and quietly trots away.

NOVEMBER

The month begins with two days of wild gales and lashing rain. In the Trap Grounds, two giant trees are down, one just narrowly missing the boardwalk; hundreds of broken willow branches lie scattered on the ground. We are slowly gathering them up, lopping and stacking them. On the stream a beautiful pair of **Teal**, our smallest wild duck, has taken shelter. A young Heron is another frequent visitor, to be seen most mornings, often just across the stream. He has become so used to passers-by on the boardwalk, he ignores them to carry on fishing.

Autumn leaf
November is often thought of as a grey month, but the glowing, flaring leaf colours, changing week by week, more than make up for it. And from time to time the sun breaks through the clouds, igniting a conflagration of reds and golds.

The weekend gales have already torn the leaves from the tallest trees. Tallest of all, the Lombardy Poplar in Foxglove meadow, which last week was a 40-metre pillar of shimmering yellow and brown, now stands leafless. Likewise the taller Ash and Chestnut trees, some of the Crack Willows, any tree that reaches above its immediate neighbours. In the gusts, the newly fallen leaves swirl across the meadows, piling in deep, crackling drifts around tree trunks, log piles, haycocks. Lower down, in contrast, the smaller trees and bushes – Hazel, Hawthorn, Dogwood, Crab Apple - are still fully clad. By the end of November, however, those branches too will be bare.

Between now and then, the leaves have their last wild fling, a glorious flush of ever-changing colours as the sap is withdrawn. The first half of November is one of the most sumptuous moments of the year: the colours richer even than the Spring. Even so, as we approach the close of Autumn, I experience the painful sense of an ending. It's the great farewell party of the growing year.

There are reds and browns, purples, scarlets and gold. Yellows predominate. And how many varied shades of yellow there are! From rich tawny, through russet and apricot, pale lemon, and flaring gold... The Hazel bushes seem to include them all: no two bushes, no two of their broad, round leaves the same. The Wild Cherries have also turned orange yellow; their long, spear-shaped leaves have a waxy sheen, tips singed with red. Our young Birch trees seem to lose their leaf-cover from the bottom up; the crown still holds its leaves in a fluttering gold filigree against the sky.

The Dogwoods sweep through an extraordinary range of colours, each bush at a different stage, every leaf different from its neighbours. I am drawn back to them day after day, as they change and flare. Just look! Some leaves have their veins outlined in yellow on a pink flush; some are pale orange; others the richest red.

COP26

The UN's international climate negotiations in Glasgow occupy the first two weeks of November, attended by representatives of around 200 nation states. The single largest group of delegates inside the Blue Zone – the core conference area – however, are lobbyists for the fossil fuel companies. They are more numerous than any national delegation. Little wonder that the international actions needed to avoid the irreversible breakdown of Earth's climate system have been postponed - yet again. We still have no end to governments' vast subsidies to fossil fuels; no carbon taxes; none of the promised aid to poor nations to mitigate the climate devastation caused by the rich; no massive investment in renewables; no comprehensive Green New Deal.

What has all this to do with the Trap Grounds? Nothing – or rather *Everything*, since all future life on earth depends on whether, and how swiftly, we can pull back from climate catastrophe and the sixth mass extinction. So: it's *everything!*

The first half of November has been largely grey and overcast, but mild: afternoon temperatures often well above 15°C. Abruptly, from mid-November, through the second half of the month we have day after day of bright sunshine, overnight frosts, daytime temperatures seldom above 7 or 8° C, often less. And with the night frosts, finally the leaves are falling, faster and faster.

Late-November work parties

Eight young volunteers from St Clare's come for their last work party of the year. They have three tasks, which they launch into with their usual cheerful energy. The first is to shovel up some soil that we have stored for years, wrapped in an enormous tarpaulin, and to spread it over the ugly heap of concrete rubble beyond the Creek, beside the Navigation Way fence. Next, they march off to Cuckoo Copse, to rake up the last of the autumn mowings and to pile them in tall haycocks. Lastly, they tackle the fallen Willow beside the boardwalk, lopping its many side branches. Now it remains for Merlin Harvey to log the main trunk with his chainsaw.

Over the next two weeks I continue their work by the Creek, burying those hideous concrete blocks under yet more soil, until I have emptied an entire one-ton bag of topsoil, sculpting the contours of the mound into smooth curves. Now it is time to plant it up. The mound lies in shade, so only shade-tolerant species like ferns and hellebores will thrive there. I seek out several of these graceful plants from hidden corners of the site: two well-grown Male Ferns, half a dozen young Hart's-tongue Ferns, a bunch of Hellebores. Carefully I dig up each one, and embed them in their new home on the mound, planting half a dozen ferns also on the opposite bank of the Creek. More are still needed; but bit by bit this former rubble heap and its surroundings is becoming a place of quiet beauty.

One evening, having finished my day's work, I am standing by the Creek in silence, savouring the last of the sunset. Just being there. Suddenly, I sense I am not alone. A big dog fox emerges only a few yards away, his red pelt flaring in the sun's dying rays. He is magnificent. Unaware of my presence, he walks slowly, confidently, right past me.

Then a twig cracks. He stops and turns towards me, gazing for a long time, but he seems unable to make me out in the shadows. So, he strolls calmly on, turning one more time to glance in my direction, before vanishing among the brambles. Go well, Brother Fox!

We have another mini work party: three young graduate students, studying sustainability, have volunteered to dig two big tree-planting holes for us. The trees – beautiful Bird Cherries – are already five feet high, so they will need deep planting holes, with room for the roots to spread. Alas, the two sites that we have chosen turn out to be encumbered with masses of concrete junk, buried well below ground level. Worse, some of those embedded concrete slabs are held together with iron reinforcing rods. I fetch our giant angle-cutter from the shed; and at last we can pull the separate slabs out of the ground. Hooray! Thank you to Katie and Paco and her other colleague who dug and prised and excavated so enthusiastically! The trees will be planted in December, hopefully to grow and flower exuberantly over many years to come.

THE END OF AUTUMN
It is the 25th of November. The succession of night frosts followed by brilliant sunlit days has continued. And each bright morning reveals fewer and fewer leaves still clinging to the branches. Even a slight breeze wafts a spiral of falling reds and golds to the ground. On the 27th of November Storm Arwen reaches Oxford: wild gales and a flurry of snow, followed by two days of pelting rain. Further North the storm has brought devastation. In northern Scandinavia, temperatures have plunged to - 40°C. Even within the gentle shelter of the Trap Grounds, more Willow branches

are down, broken twigs everywhere, the leaves ripped from the trees. The branches are bare. The long golden Autumn is at an end. The sun breaks through, but without warmth. Daytime temperatures barely struggle above 2 degrees C; sharp frosts all night.

A **Red Kite** swoops majestically overhead. Hungry.

DECEMBER

Winter is here. The month begins with frosty nights and chilly days. But now and then, when the sun breaks through, there are joyful bursts of birdsong. The **Wren** can be startlingly loud: his cascading, rippling melody echoes among the bare branches. I can see him, half hidden in the ivy, his tiny form quivering with exertion. Robins are much in evidence, too.

The weather turns mild. Even in the short grey days of December, the Trap Grounds are full of bird life, more visible now that the leaves have gone. A pair of tiny Goldcrests is active, hunting midges among the low willow branches; male blackbirds pursue one another, jockeying to establish their future breeding territories; a Siskin; a whole troop of Long-tailed Tits, perhaps the family that fledged beside Tim's Pond last April. I hear their contact calls, a gentle "zizzizzip"; I glance up, and there they are, flitting from twig to twig, a dozen small bundles of exuberant life!

By the boardwalk I catch a faint tapping. I know that sound: it's the Treecreeper. A scan of the nearest tree-trunks soon reveals that modest little bird, working its way, mouselike, up the trunk, tap, tap, tap, probing the bark for insects. From near the top, a short flight to the bottom of the next tree-trunk, and already it is working its way up. In winter it's a non-stop working day for the Treecreeper, as long as the daylight lasts.

The larger predators have more leisure time. The female Sparrowhawk rests high up in an Ash tree, taking at least half an hour to preen herself. Relaxed: she must have had breakfast already!

There is plenty on offer. Just across the railway in Burgess Field, Linnets roost in the dense bramble in flocks of three hundred or more. Redwings, late to arrive this year from Scandinavia and from Iceland, are now here in numbers too. So are the Starlings, which gather in their thousands each winter evening for their spell-binding *murmuration* on Otmoor, swirling in tight-packed clouds like Chinese dragons, before dropping into the shelter of the reed bed to sleep.

Blue Tits and Great Tits are singing. Chaffinches are about, too, but not yet singing, and not yet in their brilliant Spring plumage. Their cousins, the Goldfinches, seem to be much fewer this year. And Greenfinches, which used to be abundant, are scarcely anywhere.

Our two new Bird Cherry trees have arrived, and Paco joins me to plant them. He had already done valiant work on the planting holes, a few weeks ago. Each tree has been donated by a supporter in memory of a loved one who shared their affection for the Trap Grounds. We trundle yet more barrowloads of topsoil, then carefully plant the young saplings, back-filling around and beneath their roots with the rich soil. Each tree takes us about an hour. Grow well, little trees!

Later, I take a couple of days to excavate and then transplant three young Holly trees, and several more ferns. They stand now on both sides of the Creek, near the outflow of our slow stream. A month ago, in this same spot, I had an encouter with a big dog fox. This time I am honoured by a visit from a Muntjac deer.

December this year, after the first few days, is extraordinarily mild. Mild and wet. We have had days of torrential rain, raising the stream enough to flood in below the boardwalk.

Leading up to New Year we have record-breaking temperatures of 15-16° C. Enough to set our resident Song Thrushes singing: a preview of Spring. There are other early signs of Spring, too. A few Primroses are already in flower, as well as some Hellebores and the marzipan-scented Winter Heliotrope. The **Robin** has begun whistling his magical notes. It's the New Year. Hope is in the air.

THE TRAP GROUNDS:
A VERY BRIEF USERS' GUIDE

Here are just one or two suggestions, to start with, in case they help. Make a time to be outside – every day, if possible, however briefly – in a green space. The **Trap Grounds** is a good place to try!

Put away that mobile phone! No ear-plugs!

Wake up your senses. Stand and close your eyes. Feel the sun or the wind or the rain on your face. Listen quietly for a while: what can you hear? The rustle of leaves and grasses? The buzz of insects? Birds calling? Open your eyes again: can you spot them?

As you walk on, stop here and there to touch a tree trunk, explore its texture: ribbed or rutted or smooth. Rub a leaf between your fingers; it could be a fallen leaf or one still on the tree. How does it smell? Try different kinds of leaf or bark. Could you tell them apart, just by smell? By the shape and size of the leaves, the pattern of twigs, their blossoms, or berries?

Now, if it's Spring or Summer, try exploring the many different flowering plants in the meadows. Take your time. Squat down: look closely. Within your immediate field of view, how many kinds of plants can you see? (How many of them can you identify?) Look around. Can you spot any bees, grasshoppers, spiders, butterflies…?

＊ ＊ ＊

Before you go, find a moment to reflect on the astonishing diversity of living beings, their beauty and wonder, their intricate physiology, and the countless interweavings of the global ecosystem on which all life depends.

And remember: *You too* are a precious part of it! Your life, like that of everyone else, is interwoven with the intricate living system of planet Earth – unique, so far as we know, in the universe.

And here and now, this is a place, a realm, a world of wonder, where **you belong**.

Look after it!

CONSERVATION TASKS
ROUND THE YEAR

JANUARY/FEBRUARY
- Tree felling and pruning. Stack logs and brush as invertebrate habitat
- Cut back branches overshading ditches, ponds, and meadows
- Dig up (or cut back) brambles in open areas
- Spread gravel on muddy paths, as needed
- Plant/transplant ferns while dormant
- Rubbish blitzes

MARCH/APRIL
- Selective mowing/strimming of meadows to control coarse grass and bramble before wildflowers begin to grow. Dates (ranging from early March to mid-April) depend on when grass starts growing. Rake the hay into piles.
- Divide and plant out snowdrops, primroses, celandines (etc.) to spread them
- Pull/uproot nettles
- Mark paths through Snowdrop Glade with hooped hazel wands
- Sow seeds of later-flowering flowers

April/May

- Limit noisy or intrusive tasks during peak birds' nesting season
- Eradicate any Giant Hogweed and Japanese Knotweed (if found). Cut it down before it flowers. Dig out the roots with mattocks. Put all stems and leaves in sealed plastic bags and leave to rot.

June

- In a dry summer, water young trees and wildflowers. Continue as needed in July
- Pull up over-dominant Michaelmas Daisy, and Golden Rod. Dig up Hogweed.
- Keep paths clear of encroaching vegetation

July/August

- Collect Yellow Rattle and other seeds (free source: Milham Ford meadow)
- Book City Council's volunteers to cut a block of reeds in September
- Check ditches and watercourses for Himalayan Balsam; pull out the roots before the flowers set seeds. Continue as needed in September/October
- Skim duckweed from the ponds; rake out Parrot's Feather from Dragonfly Pond
- (Late August) Mow selected meadow areas (continued in September)

September/October

- Any dredging of ponds or watercourses is best done in early September when water levels are lowest. Book Aquatic Solutions well in advance

- Mow all remaining meadows and glades. Rake the hay and pile it in sunny spots for winter refuges
- Sow Yellow Rattle, Red Campion, and all other seeds requiring vernalisation
- Work with the Parks Department's volunteers to scythe a block of reeds (c. 400m^2).
- Check reedbed for invasive Goat Willows and other emergent scrub; engage a tree surgeon to deal with them: poison the trunks, and remove (or burn) all branches to prevent then re-rooting
- Dig out (or cut back) spreading brambles; uproot all end-rooting bramble-shoots
- Sweep leaves from boardwalk at least once a week while the leaves are falling.
- Best months for planting and transplanting bulbs (bluebells, snowdrops, etc)
- Clean bird boxes

November / December
- Transplant ferns, hellebores, iris, to spread
- (December) Plant new trees and shrubs
- Coppice hazels, and save wands for wattle fences (see March/April)
- Conduct rubbish blitzes
- Clear rotting leaves from toolshed roof and boardwalk
- Tidy shed and sharpen tools.